M.S.N

MARIA ....als. During the Second World War she was evacuated to Ireland. On return to Scotland her family moved around and finally settled in Pollok, Glasgow, where she remained until her marriage to Jim Fyfe. She now has two sons, Stephen and Chris, and four grandchildren, Catriona, Jacob, Max and Peter. Maria worked in various roles in the secretarial and education sectors before her political career, gaining a 2:1 in Economic History as a mature student. She joined the Labour Party in 1960, where (after a 'wasted year' in Jim Sillars' Scottish Labour Party) she has remained ever since. Maria was a Glasgow District Councillor from 1980 to 1987 and them Glasgow Maryhill's MP from 1987 until she retired in 2001. Since rtirement, Maria has remained politically active, most recently in the successful Mary Barbour campaign. She was awarded an Honorary Doctorate by Glasgow University for her work for women.

By the Same Author:
A Problem Like Maria: A Woman's Eye View of Life as an MP, Luath Press, 2014
Women Saying No (ed.), Luath Press, 2014

Singing in the Streets

A Glasgow Memoir

MARIA FYFE

Luath Press Limited

EDINBURGH

www.luath.co.uk

First published 2020

ISBN: 978-1-913025-70-0

The paper used in this book is recyclable. It is made from low chlorine pulps produced in a low energy, low emission manner from renewable forests.

Printed and bound by Bell & Bain Ltd, Glasgow

Typeset in 11.5 point Sabon LT Pro by Carrie Hutchison

Contents

*For Catriona, Jacob, Max and Peter, who
make their grandmother so proud.*

Acknowledgements

My thanks go out to Tom Brown and Jim Cassidy for their useful professional advice; Malky Burns, Ian Davidson, Johann Lamont, Gus Macdonald, Jim Mackechnie, Des McNulty and Bob Winter for their memories of times past and/or useful comments; Lorna Miller for her permission to use her wonderful artwork on the cover of this book; Gavin MacDougall, Carrie Hutchison and the team at Luath Press; and Don and Eileen Macdonald, my hugely caring neighbours, who not only brought our local community together, entertaining with music when we were out clapping on Thursday nights for the NHS and carers, but kept me supplied with my regular newspapers, which kept me sane while the lockdown held me indoors.

The Cover

LORNA MILLER has been causing trouble and entertainment with her cartoons and artwork since childhood and has been lucky to make it her career for the past 27 years. She is the only woman in the UK to have a weekly political cartoon with *Bella Caledonia* and she also works for the *Guardian*. She is regularly commissioned as a campaign Artist & Designer for UNISON, GMB, STUC and Common Weal. Lorna has been involved with environmental campaigns, autism and disability awareness and most recently as a member of Long Covid Scotland Action Group, having suffered ongoing health issues due to the virus. She is @mistressofline on Instagram and Twitter. www.lornamiller.com

The cover image brings together Glasgow women across the decades who fought for equality through the Trade Union Movement. Mary McArthur, on the left, was a suffragette who had rebelled against her Tory family to become chair of the Ayr branch of the Shop Assistants' Union. By 1903 she was the first woman on its national executive board.

Standing beside her is Agnes McLean who led the strike for equal pay in 1943 and 1969. She was a formidable character with great style who loved to dance the rumba.

On the right, representing the successful Glasgow Equal Pay Strike, Is Denise Phillips a UNISON activist and Homecarer.

The image was originally commissioned by Glasgow Trades Council for the 2018 May Day poster.

Preface

BACK IN 1958 a gem of a book about growing up in Glasgow was published. That book was Cliff Hanley's *Dancing in the Streets*. As a 19 year old Glasgow girl I lapped up every page of it (I have always shared his Glaswegian nationalism). As a schoolgirl I had daydreamed of being a reporter, and here was this guy doing it with wit and wisdom. Back then women didn't get to be reporters, except for food, fashion and furnishings. I earned a few pounds with such freelance work, but my heart wasn't in it.

I found myself steered in a different direction. Labour was defeated in the 1959 General Election for the third time and I read my first ever political paperback, *Must Labour Lose?*. I felt this could not possibly be. The party that got my parents out of the tenements and into a high quality, well-built council house with gardens back and front? The party that had created the NHS, meaning no more counting coins to pay doctors' bills? Like many other youngsters at the time, I decided to join the party and see if I could do anything to help. Cliff Hanley himself had joined the Independent Labour Party and taken part in soapbox oratory.

In similar circumstances today, it seems a good time to recount another childhood, that of a girl growing up in Glasgow, and tell the story of how the decision to join the Labour Party led to unexpected consequences. Hanley introduced his book quoting Groucho Marx's declamation, 'Let there be dancing in the streets, drinking in the saloons and necking in the parlours.' But why leave out singing? I was to enjoy plenty experiences of singing outdoors and indoors. 'The Internationale' and 'The Red Flag', obviously. Trade union songs like 'Joe Hill'. Umpteen folk songs. A whole playbook of Campaign for Nuclear Disarmament (CND) songs. Songs about the Irish rebellion – much to my parents' annoyance. Later on, 'Nkosi Sikelel iAfrika', in support of the Anti-Apartheid struggle.

It seems obvious that this book should be titled *Singing in the Streets*. My earlier book, *A Problem Like Maria*, recounts my experiences in Parliament, good and bad, marvellous and insufferable. I've often been asked what I did before entering Parliament. Having spent seven years as a councillor in Glasgow, I think younger people especially, downcast at the result of the 2019 General Election, might like to know how we, the Left, fought back against Margaret Thatcher. We cannot wallow in misery. We have to fight. And part of that is getting our facts straight.

Let's look at Scotland first. Ours is the only nation in the UK where the Tories lost MPs and vote share. The SNP message was 'Stop Johnson' which was clear and simple, while Labour's was an attempt to bring Brexiteers and Remainers together. But the simple arithmetic of the matter is that the SNP could not keep Johnson out of Number 10, even if they won every single constituency in Scotland. And the more they talked of an alliance with Labour with that end in mind, the more it reminded people of the Tory poster putting Ed Miliband in Alex Salmond's pocket.

Johnson being Prime Minister is proving to be a good recruiting sergeant for the SNP. But scepticism remains amongst much of the public, and no amount of Saltire-waving will answer questions like how an independent Scotland would handle trade and customs arrangements with England when it is out of the EU and if Scotland rejoins. It's hard to see how any updated White Paper can answer this until after the UK–EU trade talks are completed.

As for Labour, a renewal of Better Together seems extremely unlikely, and I am surprised to see it mooted at all. The Tories are even more right-wing than in Thatcher's day. Witness the likes of Kenneth Clark and Michael Heseltine urging people not to vote Tory. No, remembering our roots is the answer to revival. Remember Mary Barbour's army and take heart.

During the First World War private landlords pushed up the rents, calculating the women would be a soft touch with the men being away in the trenches. They didn't reckon with Mary Barbour.

She and twenty thousand women refused to pay higher rent, their campaign culminating in a huge demonstration when some tenants were taken to court. Lloyd George, then munitions minister, told the court to drop the charges and a few months later the government passed the first law forcing rents back to pre-war levels. And these women did not even have the vote. Mary went on to pursue many more reforms: free, pure school milk, wash houses, public baths, mother and baby clinic, and the first women's health advice clinic; all much needed when women often gave birth to large families while suffering tuberculosis.

The Labour movement is well aware of our male heroes. In today's world I'd like to see them not simply revered, but listened to. They have lessons for today.

England delivered for the Tories – 345 out of their total of 365 seats. Yet there were mixed results. The north of England saw seats like Bolsover being lost to the Tories. But the right-wing media didn't mention Labour held all the seats in Liverpool, Leeds, Newcastle and Sheffield. These cities too had had their share of being 'left behind'. Is the explanation that city dwellers are more cosmopolitan in outlook?

Conclusion: learn from history. In 1931 Labour was down to 52 MPs, a huge drop from 248 in 1929. Ramsay MacDonald, the Labour Prime Minister, was expelled for setting up a 'national' government largely peopled by Tories. Yet by 1945 it was able to win a landslide in that election for ambitious plans undeterred by the state of the nation's finances. Surprisingly, it is the case that in our 2019 election, Labour won 10,300,000 votes. That is more than was won by either Ed Miliband or Gordon Brown. Whenever Labour's death is yet again announced, I am always reminded of Mark Twain, on reading news he had died, commenting, 'The report of my death was an exaggeration.'

And here's another surprising statistic. For years I wondered when, if ever, we would achieve equal representation of Labour women in Parliament. Well, it's happened – 104 women MPs out of a 203 total. And some of them are already showing they are up for a fight.

Chapter 1

War Baby

PERHAPS CROSSING THE U-boat infested Irish Sea with three young children was not the best idea my mother ever had. Our vessel was one of several travelling in a convoy escorted by destroyers. Anyone might think that seeing all these ships equipped with guns lined up before setting sail would make anyone think twice. Not her. It was 1941 and earlier that year Hitler had announced he would sink every ship that came within 60 miles of any Irish port. In the first six months of that year nearly three million tonnes of shipping were sunk by U-boats, so small and low lying they were hard to see even if they were above water.

I was a toddler, the youngest of the three children. No fewer than three kind-hearted sailors took turns to hold me safely as the steamer bucketed its way over to Larne, while my mother was throwing up over the side. Hence my lifelong admiration for sailors. It was not as if all she had to do was go and buy the tickets at the Burns Laird office. Permission had to be sought, and she waited months to get the go ahead. No-on asked her the famous wartime question, 'Is your journey really necessary?' For it really was not. There were plenty of safe places in rural mainland Britain where children were being evacuated. At least at home there were air raid shelters. An attack at sea would probably end in drowning.

In fact, we had already experienced evacuation inland, just before the war started, when Hitler invaded Poland. Children were being evacuated for fear that towns like Glasgow would be razed by German bombers. Nothing did happen at that stage and we all returned home after only three weeks because my mother could not stand another minute of the condescending manner of the chatelaine of the Earl of Inchcape's castle near Ballantrae, where we had been accommodated along with four other families from Glasgow. Whatever it was exactly the peer's wife did or said that annoyed my mother I never learned, but it must have been quite something to make her prefer to risk life and limb to being patronised.

So why make this journey to Ireland? Glasgow was being bombed again and again. The worst bombing nights were on 13 and 14 March 1941, and the Gorbals, so near the docks and the shipyards, took a pounding on many a night. It must have been hellish, getting through those long hours, night after night in the air raid shelter, waiting for the all-clear and wondering if your home was still intact. Clydebank, only a few miles down the river, was blitzed to all but total destruction on those nights in March, leaving only seven houses out of a total of 12,000 still standing undamaged. I can see all too clearly why my mother wanted to get out of Glasgow without delay. She perhaps had other reasons. At that time my brothers Jim and Joe were only attending school two or three half days a week because St John's Primary had no air raid shelter. She might have been aware that no such problem existed over in Ireland. There was also a lot of concern expressed at the time that infants, too young to understand what was going on, might get a 'complex' because of the fear engendered by the Blitz. I don't remember being afraid, but I've spoken to a few contemporaries about this period, and we have something in common. Whenever we hear, in a war film or documentary, the air raid warning siren a shiver runs up our spines. Our air raid shelter was in the basement of the Co-operative Stores in Bridge Street, around the corner. We often had to stay all night through, until the all-clear sounded and we could go home.

And what part of Ireland were we headed to? A small town on the west coast called Bundoran. Why there? The obvious answer might have been that Ireland was neutral, and no one had any motive to bomb the Donegal coastline. Yet apparently her reason was simply that she knew Bundoran well already, as that was where her family roots were, and she had a bachelor grand-uncle Henry living there in a thatched cottage on the cliff edge about a mile south of Bundoran. My brother Jim had been intended to inherit the croft, and in recognition of this honour his confirmation name, Bartholomew, was a compliment to Henry's elder brother of that name. But Tholm, as he was known, died, and Henry mortgaged the croft so he and his cronies could drink the proceeds.

In the summer of 1941 Henry was still very much with us. The family had made frequent visits before the war, so it was a wonder he agreed to let us over the door again. Joe, on entering the cottage door for the first time, when he was an observant if somewhat forthright toddler, had disbelievingly seen the hens allowed to run in and out, and remarked, 'Whit a durty hoose.'

'What did the child say?' asked Henry.

'He said it was a lovely house.'

'Naw Ah didnae...'

'Wheesht!'

Henry was small, gnarled and white haired, and becoming st-ooped and not as strong as he used to be. There was no running water in the cottage, so Jim and Joe helped him by fetching it in buckets from a nearby stream.

We didn't remain long in the cottage. Mum found that tongues wagged in the neighbourhood at the idea of this young woman staying unchaperoned in the house of a single man, even if he had one foot in the grave, and so she sought accommodation in one of the cheaper hotels, aided by the allowance for evacuees' accommodation paid by the wartime government.

Jim had just turned old enough for secondary school in Bundoran. What my mother had not known when she hurried us out of Scotland was that the Irish government's policy was that all such pupils had to be taught Irish Gaelic. My mother saw no point in that as she believed optimistically we would be going home soon anyway. So she home-schooled Jim herself, no mean feat considering she had left school at 14. When we returned to Glasgow Jim was advanced a year.

Joe was sent to the small local primary school where he settled in happily enough at first. Then one day one of the boys in his class spat at him, and Joe retaliated by poking him in the eye. The teacher got a heavy walking stick out of his drawer to belabour him, but not the original culprit. 'I'm not having that,' said Joe, and walked out, never to return. One day I was sitting on a stone wall on the road to Bundoran while Jim was patiently trying to persuade a reluctant donkey to give me a ride. The donkey gave him a dismissive kick. Then one of the local lads came along the street and jeered, 'Aw, look at the big Jessie, minding his wee sister.' Before Jim could draw breath I yelled back, 'Scram, stupid appearance!' The lad was so surprised that he did. I've no idea where I got this phrase from. All his life Jim told people about it. He was proud of his fearless wee sister. Ignorance is bliss, more like. Then, when I became an MP, he told people I would put up a good fight if I could see off big boys when I was only two.

We returned to Scotland after nine months in Bundoran, unable to get back any earlier because by then strict wartime travel restrictions were being enforced. My mother had been distraught at being refused permission to travel across the sea to attend her mother's funeral in the August of 1941. Understandable, but it could easily have been her own funeral – and ours – as well.

Meanwhile my dad, who had stayed at home to keep the wages coming in, was driving his tram throughout the Blitz and coming home night after night to an empty, unheated, cheerless flat without complaint. One night an elderly lady dropped a bag full of groceries when she was boarding his tram at Charing Cross and took an age to collect all the items from the wet street. He was muttering to himself with impatience as he helped her gather her bits and pieces together, because the driver could be disciplined if he was more than two minutes late. And the resulting holdup did make him late getting to Kelvingrove. Lucky for him. A land mine struck just when his tram should have been passing through.

If we had not escaped the U-boats I would not have reached my third birthday. But I had another piece of good fortune when I was born. A few years before the Second World War broke out, the infant mortality rate in Glasgow was exceptionally poor. It was the worst in Europe. You can be sure if that was how it was for the whole of Glasgow, then the Gorbals was worse. Yet I was born in robust health, with such an appetite for my mother's milk my brothers immediately dubbed me 'the bottomless pit'. Our family lived in a gas-lit room-and-kitchen in a tenement in Bedford Street, a main artery through the Gorbals.

The lavatory was exactly that. A toilet pan. No washbasin. A chain, too far up for me to reach, hung down from the cistern high up on the wall. This lavatory was on an outside staircase and shared with two other households on our landing. The next door neighbour had Irish lodgers, so there could be a queue of seven or eight standing around waiting. The rent was 9s (45 pence) a month. We lived there because our mother wanted to be near her own mother, who lived upstairs.

I was nine months old when the Second World War broke out in Europe, and when I was two I thought the bombs were coming when we were merely hurrying out of the rain. Everyone who was a young child at that time remembers their Mickey Mouse gas mask, but when you are a baby or a small infant you needed something specially designed to prevent tiny hands, in ignorance of what they were doing, pushing the mask aside. There was such an invention, and you can see it in Glasgow's People's Palace, the city's much-loved social history museum, to this day. It consisted of a bag big enough to hold an infant body, the gas mask itself, and a wide clear panel to allow the baby to see out. My mother had to carry it everywhere she went with me in case there was a gas attack.

If we went out at night we needed a torch, taped over so that only a tiny pinpoint of light showed us our way in the blackout, but I was not afraid when I had my two big brothers to swing me along. At ten and eight years old, there was a big age gap between them and me when I was born. Both my brothers were black haired, like all the family, and tall for their age, but otherwise quite different in character and appearance. Jim was very lean, studious, responsible and hardworking – a typical eldest child. Joe was sturdier, very sporty and not likely to do his homework if he could get away with winging it. But to my toddler mind, both were equally to be relied upon. A favourite ploy of mine was to jump off the kitchen table without warning, in the absolute certainty that one or other would catch me.

The darkness in the street outside meant you had to watch where you were going on the uneven pavement. Besides, a bogeyman might be hiding up a close waiting to grab you and carry you away. Jim and Joe would shout 'Boo!' as we passed the entrance to a tenement to scare off any bogeyman that might jump out at me.

At birth I was registered as Catherine Mary O'Neill, but when I was baptised a few days afterwards the priest, speaking the words of the ceremony in Latin, instead of 'Mary' said 'Maria'. My parents, not usually ones for snap decisions, instantly decided they liked this better, and so I have a name that is common enough amongst the peasantry in Latin countries, but not so common amongst the plebeians of Scotland. Parents really should be careful about their children's initials. Mine, forming the letters 'C', 'M', 'O', 'N', inspired my uncle Johnny, my mother's elder brother, to hail me, 'C'mon, C'mon', whenever he saw me, putting me in a foot stamping rage. Dad's father, named Daniel, was born in Kilrea, a small village in Co. Londonderry. Sometime around the late 1880s, when they were in their teens, he and his two older brothers were instructed by their dad to take a cow to market, but instead of going back home with the proceeds, they bought tickets for the steamer and headed to Glasgow. Their mother had died, and when their father married again they disliked their stepmother so much that this seemed their only solution. There was many a family story told about Daniel. He was blacklisted for rousing fellow workers to join a trade union when he worked in an ironworks in the east end. The union, small and poorly organised in those early efforts to represent unskilled workers, went bust. So did the company, when the striking workers brought production to a halt.

Then there was the time one Mr Healy, a wealthy man who owned a chain of ham and egg shops, a specialty common in those days, offered the local branch of the Ancient Order of Hibernians a £5 prize – a great deal of money in those days – for some competition or other. Granddad stood up at a packed meeting in their hall that night and expressed his concerns forcefully. 'We cannot accept this money,' he declared, 'until Mr Healy pays decent wages to his shop staff.' The ensuing row broke up the organisation and I grew up wanting to be like my grandfather. My mother had Donegal roots, and her maiden surname was Lacey. She believed she was descended from one of the sailors with the Spanish Armada who had either been shipwrecked or had decided his sailing days were over and sought haven ashore there. Her coal-black hair and large brown eyes seemed to bear witness to this possibility. Having fallen out with all her in-laws by the time I was an infant, she would say, 'Just like an O'Neill' every time I did something to annoy her.

I never knew my mother's parents, my mother's mother having died when I was only two. I was told she had a crooked little finger, which came about from working in the Dundee jute mills from about 12 years of age – a common minor disfigurement amongst mill lassies, that came about from using their pinkie to catch threads at an age when their hands were not yet fully developed. She always wore cotton or wool gloves when she went out and made a point of never wearing a shawl. In her day shawls were seen as a badge of poverty. Owen Lacey, my mother's father, had a habit of standing on the corner steps of a local bank, chatting with his cronies, and that is all I remember of him. With his walrus moustache, cloth bunnet, and pipe stuck in his mouth, he looked just like Paw Broon. He worked as a stoker and ship's greaser with the P&O Line for many years, on ships travelling to ports around the Far East, and that must have been physically demanding.

I never saw either of my father's parents. Daney died before I was born. Although she never saw my brothers and me all these years, my paternal grandmother must have kept a place for us in her heart, because when she died in 1953, when I was 14, she left sums of money to us in her will. She had saved up her entire dividend over all the years of her membership of the Co-operative since the day she became a married woman, and it amounted to some £2,000, a small fortune in those days. Our shares bought suits for my brothers Jim and Joe, and my first grown up 'costume' bought at Pettigrew & Stephens in Sauchiehall Street. The grey wool jacket was fitted, the skirt accordion pleated and a new lemon blouse from a shop in the Argyll Arcade completed the ensemble. Whenever I went out in my new outfit, and in my first pair of Louis heel shoes, I felt a million dollars.

I wish I had known this granny to whom I owed such largesse. For years I had no idea why I never saw her. I had known about the estrangement since I was about ten years old, when I was rooting one day through the shoe box that held the family photographs. There was my parents' wedding picture, my dad in a dark suit, my mother wearing a knee length straight white satin shift with a long lampshade fringe at the hem and carrying a huge bouquet of white lilies and roses. Her bridesmaid, her sister Mary, sat at her side. But a rough tear all the way down the right hand side of the picture showed someone was missing.

'Who was that in the picture?' I asked.

'That was your uncle Patrick,' Mum said. 'He was your dad's best man.'

'But why was he torn out?'

'I'll tell you when you're old enough,' she said.

I waited many years to be told. Meanwhile I wondered what on earth he could have done. Was he a child molester? A murderer? A rapist? A spy for Germany?

It was on my 32nd birthday when we were reminiscing at the fireside about the family, that she finally decided I might now be old enough to hear. As we sat together on the sofa in a grave tone of voice she said, 'One day your dad was a bit late getting back from work, and Patrick came round to visit. He often dropped in. Only this time he had a drink in him, and he tried to make a pass at me.'

I waited for her to go on, and when she remained silent I asked, 'So what happened next?'

'Nothing really. Drunk as he was, he soon realised he wasn't on. I pushed him away, and told him to get out, and he went. It was all over in a moment or two.'

'And that was it? Is that it?' I squawked.

Mum frowned in puzzlement and disbelief at my reaction. I had to tell her that compared to what I had been imagining all those years this seemed, well, not a lot to worry about. I think if it had happened to me I would have been angry, but if he had apologised I would have put it down to the demon drink, while still being careful of ever being alone with him. And of course, my dad had every right to be angry with his brother. But a lifelong vendetta, keeping grandparents and children apart? It doesn't seem reasonable to me. However, I have lately wondered what did my mother mean by a 'pass'? Defined in my dictionary as amorous or sexual advances, that can cover quite a range from the mildly flirtatious to the gross.

I hasten to add, in fairness to a man who cannot answer for himself from beyond the grave, that I have only ever heard my mother's account of this incident, not my long deceased uncle's. In any case, there were already existing tensions that this matter brought to a head. Mum just didn't like her in-laws. No, that's wrong. She loathed them. She saw Dad's sister Sarah as schoolteachery and supercilious, and Patrick had put himself beyond the pale.

My mother was a pretty woman, with a heart-shaped face. She disliked having a slightly upturned nose, but when she read in some women's magazine that this shape was called 'retroussée' she felt better about it. Her black hair fell easily into waves. With wearisome repetitiveness she told me year in year out that a woman's crowning glory was her hair. When I was a wee girl and wanting to get out to play, mutinously fretting as she curled my hair with heated tongs, it would promptly revert to being straight as soon as I was outdoors in our damp climate. In my late teenage years, she told me that, with poker straight hair like mine, I would really spoil my chances of getting a boyfriend. When I pointed out that observation of couples in the street disproved this theory, she would sigh and say I was being irritatingly logical. Just like an O'Neill.

My parents were disgusted by Alexander McArthur's novel, *No Mean City*, a bestseller that painted a dreadful picture of Glasgow, full of razor gangs, seedy sex scenes, and general squalor. Yet the reality of my parents' and their neighbours' lives was scrubbing the walls to make sure bugs were kept at bay, and taking turns to wash down the tenement stairs. The violence and criminal ongoings were simply not how those Catholic, Protestant and Jewish families lived. When youngsters of my brothers' generation went out into the wider world, they met people who only knew of the Gorbals what they had read in that book, and it did damage to the city's reputation – and its citizens' job chances – that took decades to overcome.

Before her marriage, my mother had been the manager of a licensed grocer's shop in the Gorbals, but she gave up work when she got married. It was considered a blow to a man's pride if his wife worked. She even felt compelled to give up her membership of St John's Church choir. She enjoyed singing – she was always singing about the house. But a married woman – even if she was not yet a mother – had to concentrate on her domestic duties and have no time for fripperies like singing in a choir. I am certain this notion did not come from any diktat of my dad's. That wasn't in his nature.

When she was a teenager her father bought her a second-hand accordion at The Barras (Glasgow's famous street market) and she taught herself to play it. When she sang around the house it was more often Irish ballads than anything else. Songs from the music hall, like 'She's Only a Bird in a Gilded Cage' are hard wired into my own memory, but when I heard her sing 'If I Had a Talking Picture of You' I was puzzled. Pictures hung on the wall didn't talk. Mum thought this was hilarious, because of course the song was about 'the talkies' at the cinema.

During the Depression, before I was born, she and Dad had created a concert party they named 'The Sunbeams', when he was out of work for four years. Its members were the children of his local branch of the Knights of St Columba, a Catholic charitable organisation. They trained the kids to dance, sing and recite poetry, and the idea was they would perform free, but with a slap-up tea to follow, at fundraising events around greater Glasgow. The tea, of course, was a welcome incentive to cash-strapped families. One girl had a costume for every dance. Be it flamenco, Egyptian sand dance, Cossack, no matter how exotic, her indefatigable mother would run it up on her sewing machine. The sad thing was, her daughter had little talent, so my dad had to exercise great diplomacy while Mum, who could be a little too tactless, stayed out the way. I still have a photo of two of their star performers – Cox and Cusick – in their dancing outfits. Long after my parents gave this up men and women would stop my mother in the street, calling out 'Auntie Peggy!' and reminisce about their performances. If any of those artistes ever made it to the stage I'd love to know.

My dad had the good fortune during the Depression to get a part time job as hall keeper for the Knights, paying 15s a week, not declared to the 'Buroo' (the unemployment bureau). The hall was used for weddings, funerals, and all sorts of celebrations, so there were often some leftovers to supplement the miserly dole money. Whenever, after the Depression was over, Dad was in funds he sometimes brought home a box of Black Magic chocolates for Mum. This was a standing family joke, because the first ever time he did so was when he broke the news he had been sacked. Mum was always suspicious of bad news when she saw this particular brand of chocs emerge from the brown paper bag.

My mother's other notable talent was sewing. She often made outfits for me on her ancient black and gold second-hand table-top Singer sewing machine. She would push the material under the needle as it rose up and down again with her left hand while 'ca'in the haunle' (turning the handle manually) to control the speed with her right. If the material was very fine, and needed extra careful guidance underneath the needle, I was called upon to turn the handle gently and slowly. My other job was to thread the needle to get her going, as her own eyesight wasn't up to it. Then there was the problem of comprehending the patterns, some of which were unbelievably complex. Lewis's Polytechnic in Argyle Street, where Debenham's now stands, had a large department devoted to the sale of dressmaking material and patterns for all kinds of clothes. I was always glad when she chose a Butterick pattern. I could understand their instructions. But *Vogue* – although ultra-fashionable – was usually beyond our collective wits. We were all baffled by the instruction in one such pattern to use tailors' tacks. My mother asked for them in half a dozen different shops, and no-one had heard of them. Until one day, an assistant, who could hardly tell her for laughing, revealed that tailors' tacks were simply long hand stitches used to hold the hem in place so that the machine stitching could be done more easily.

A sailor suit, made for me when I was four, was created despite these setbacks. I had the traditional sailor's tunic with the squared-off collar hanging down at the back, a white lanyard hanging down my front, a navy blue accordion pleated skirt and a sailor's cap set jauntily on my head, its band braided with the name of some Royal Navy ship HMS *Something-or-Other*. She had seen the braid in the window of an armed forces' outfitters in Jamaica Street, and fibbed that her husband was serving aboard that vessel. I liked my sailor suit a lot. The item I hated was my brown gabardine raincoat, which I deliberately left in the school cloakroom, in the hope of its being stolen by some other pupil. It was. No-one could have mis-taken it for the usual shop-bought 'utility' raincoat, which were all identical. I suppose I was just uncomfortable at being different. But my mother was not going to have her handiwork lost so easily. She stood in wait at the school gates, caught the culprit, and had a few acerbic words with her mother before bringing her trophy home.

Clothes were rationed in 1941, and your limit was 66 coupons in a year. Advertisements would show the price of the garment and the number of coupons needed: it was 26 for a man's suit, three for children's shoes. For many years my dad used a cobbler's last, the better to grip a worn out shoe when he mended it with leather soles bought from Woolworths. As late as 1949 – four years after the war ended – my primary class was taught to darn the heels in socks and elbows in cardigans. We were even made to make ourselves a pair of knickers with a remnant of cotton and some elastic. The hems on girls' dresses would be at least three or four inches, so that they could be let down as they grew.

My recollection of wartime food shortages is not a remembrance of deprivation. But one particular day sticks in my mind: the day my mother tried to get me to eat a boiled egg. Egg, in my experi-ence, was a powder that came out of a cardboard box. With all the conservatism that children can display towards unknown foods, I resisted it. Mum was actually crying as she tried to persuade me to eat the egg because she was worried about my low growth rate, but this was maternal over-anxiety. I was bouncing with health. She met my refusal with the threat of the 'jandies', a terrible illness that would turn my skin yellow and stop me from running about and playing. It was years before I realised she was talking about jaundice. Finally, she won me over by mashing it with margarine in a teacup, one teaspoonful for my teddy bear, one for me, until it was done.

Rationing was introduced in 1940. Meat of any kind available was limited to 1s 2d worth (around 5.8 pence now) for every person per week. At early 1940s prices that would buy half a pound of mince.

Sweets had special coupons of their own at the back of the ration book. You got a mere six ounces every four weeks, and this scarcity lasted until 1953. At least it kept caries at bay. Back then, if you couldn't get any toothpaste, you put soot from the chimney on your toothbrush.

Shops were told to fix their prices in line with government guidelines, so that no-one would go hungry. A contrast to the First World War, when many shops fixed their prices so high that only the better off could afford to buy.

There was National Margarine in half pound blocks that came in a plain greaseproof paper wrapper – brand names did not exist. Butter came in a large mound from which the assistant would cut off a piece and, with the aid of wooden paddles, knock it into an approximate rectangular shape before wrapping it in greaseproof paper. If you wanted cheddar cheese the assistant would take a wire cutter to a large block and assess the exact place to cut to provide the desired amount.

Vegetables like carrots and potatoes were never seen in plastic packs but came loose and with the earth still sticking to them. Bacon was sliced to the thickness you required. Sugar was scooped into small paper bags. Items like potatoes were borne home in string bags. People held on to their supplies of paper and unpicked the knots in string. There were no plastic carrier bags. You had to queue to be served by a grocery assistant who fetched everything you wanted from the shelves behind. In those days there was no such thing as a trolley, the only aisle was in the church, there was no muzak and no-one had heard of a supermarket.

Chapter 2

'Yes! We Have No Bananas'

'YES! WE HAVE No Bananas' was a popular wartime song, expressing cheerful resignation to queuing for potatoes and having no imported fruit.

By the time I was four we had moved to a tenement in Govanhill Street, away from the Gorbals but still on the south side of the city. A big improvement. There were bright electric lights in the house – no more sputtering gas lamps – AND our own inside toilet. A large wooden bunker held the coal for the black leaded kitchen range.

At the bottom of our street was Cathcart Road, where my dad drove his tram from Langside Depot, a step away from the Victoria Infirmary. He would sometimes pop me on board and take me up and down his route. The trams in earlier days had simply been painted with a broad red, blue, green or white stripe from end to end of the upper deck according to their destination, but by that time, with the growth of the network, they had acquired numbers as well. Rouken Glen Park on the south side could be reached by tram, either from Riddrie in the east end or Gairbraid Avenue in faraway Maryhill, in the north-west of the city. If you were a south sider, Maryhill could have been on another planet, for all the likelihood of your ever going there. Little did I think in those childhood days that one day I would be the MP for Maryhill.

In summer, as I sat on the top deck in the small compartment above the driver's platform, I would hear the tree branches swish against the tram's roof and, as we approached Rouken Glen, I could look down at the bungalows with sloping front gardens filled with flowers I could not name – a magical sight to me, used as I was to muddy back courts without a blade of grass to be seen. Some had rockeries filled with tiny plants. Climbing plants with big purple flowers – clematis, probably – grew up their walls. And oh, the sight of pink and red roses round some of the doors! I wanted to buy a house like that for my mum and dad when I grew up.

The park itself was a delight, with its waterfall and formal rose garden, where I always wanted to step closer and poke my nose in to smell the wondrous scents, but equally joyful was running around the field of buttercups almost as high as myself. I would make myself a necklace by linking daisies together or hold a buttercup underneath my chin: if it glowed it meant you liked butter.

Just a short walk up Victoria Road, near where we lived, were the massive iron gates of Queen's Park, where the hawthorns bloomed pink and white in May, and still do. There were concerts in the bandstand, where performers did the splits and Cossack dances. Boys and girls out playing in the street would practise Cossack dancing: squatting down on their hunkers, back erect, arms folded across their chests and kicking out the right leg, then the left, but hardly anyone was loose-limbed enough to do the splits. But what was this, coming on stage now? A wee girl about my own age, the audience cooing at the sight of her blonde curls and frilly seashell-pink dress, who began to dance and sing Shirley Temple's 'On the Good Ship Lollipop'. I sat there scowling, wishing it would be over soon, while my mum smiled indulgently at this sweet little lass's performance. I never did like Shirley Temple. Those curls all over her head were just an aggravation to any girl of like age who had to suffer daily getting her hair primped to copy her. Off she pranced at last, and a big man came on to sing 'Don't Fence Me In'. That was more like it.

That Easter Sunday I rolled a painted cardboard egg down the hill towards the bandstand, and as I ran to retrieve it I fell and cut my knee. I had to go to the nearby 'Vickie' – the Victoria Infirmary – to get my wound dressed with iodine and 'be a brave soldier', just like the man in army uniform sitting there in the treatment room. And I'm not kidding. Iodine hurts like hell. He was gritting his teeth, so I tried not to cry too. My reward was a sweetie, but I noticed he didn't get any.

American soldiers, in their elegant uniforms and caps shaped just like chip pokes sitting jauntily on their heads, often lounged around the park gates, offering chewing gum to any passing children, saying, 'Want any gum, chum?' I wanted to hear them talk, but Mum dragged me on and wouldn't let me take any. I couldn't understand why she wouldn't stand a little while and chat with them when they spoke to her. She seemed to talk for ages with everyone else she met.

When the ration books were issued my mother hit on a good wheeze to ensure a healthier diet for her family. Vegetarians were allowed a wider range of nutritious food than meat eaters, so she claimed Dad was a vegetarian and we shared out the meat allocation for four amongst the five of us. There weren't nearly as many vegetarians around in those days as there are now, and it would have been considered more than a little faddish. One of George Orwell's essays made out sandal-wearing vegetarians to be wildly eccentric. My parents seem to have had advanced views on nourishment for their time. Dad regularly brought home as much fruit as he could carry before wartime made them scarce. Our furniture was sparse, and less up to date than our neighbours', but we were well fed, and of course, being a war baby, I had enough free, state-provided cod liver oil and orange juice poured down me to sink a battleship.

Sweets stayed rationed right up until the early '50s. The weekly amount was small, but you could save up your coupons for a binge at the cinema. Accustomed as we are nowadays to seeing piles of Easter eggs, in great variety and lavishly packaged, on display in every supermarket soon after Christmas is over, the older generations can remember when you could search Glasgow east to west, and there wouldn't be one chocolate Easter egg to be seen when the limited supplies ran out. So we painted designs on hard boiled eggs and rolled them instead. Or, if your parents could afford it, you got a cardboard egg painted with a picture of an Easter bunny or daffodils, that would contain a small packet of dolly mixtures, jelly babies or chocolates.

Rationing was the only way to ensure everyone got a fair share of whatever food was going. The land army made the most of whatever cultivable land was available, and city girls – who in civilian life were hairdressers and shop assistants – spent long hours doing hard, arduous work on our farms to release men for the armed forces.

People who had allotments or gardens were famously urged to 'Dig for Victory', but our island depended on imports a great deal, and men were losing their lives in the convoys bringing food across the Atlantic. The system had its weaknesses – a black market thrived – but I was astonished many years later to hear the uncle of a friend (at a party in the home of the first Conservative family I had encountered) argue, 'It had all been a needless bureaucracy.' What did he mean? He went on, waving his arm airily as he sat at the piano, 'We had an army of civil servants that surely had better things to do than check coupons when our country was under threat of invasion.' I was unable to politely keep quiet and was the only one in the room to offer him an argument, 'But fair shares for all would have kept up morale, and that would surely have mattered for the war effort?' He then surprised me even further, saying, 'There have never been, and never will be, fair shares for all. Give some people money today, and it will be out of their pockets tomorrow. They can't spend wisely, and they'd rather have instant gratification than save. So, there's no point in trying to create equality. It can never work.'

As I went home, heaving with indignation and bafflement that an apparently otherwise sane and humane person should hold such a view, I couldn't wait to discuss it with Dad. Dad just said, placidly puffing at his pipe, 'Never forget there are a lot of people out there who think like that, and they have votes too.'

My infant school classroom at Holy Cross Primary had a statue of Our Lady of Lourdes, in white robe and blue cloak, on the windowsill, with vases of flowers, brought in by the children each Monday, on either side. We always began the school day with prayers, standing turned facing towards the statue, eyes shut reverentially, and hands closed flat together with thumbs crossed. We sat in rows of wooden desks made for two, all facing the front, and we could keep our play piece on a shelf underneath. The teacher spoke to all of us together and we sat up straight at attention, but I noticed that if a boy or girl put a hand up they were allowed to leave the room. I tentatively experimented with this and found that I too was given the nod to go. It hadn't occurred to me that my classmates were seeking permission to go to the toilet. I promptly headed for home, across the busy traffic, and went straight to my back court to play. My mother did not even know I was there until she heard my voice from her kitchen window. So, hauled back to school, I was told I must stay there until the janitor rang his hand bell and Mum would come and collect me. But suppose he forgot to ring the bell? That was a worry.

My misunderstandings did not stop there. We had begun to learn the alphabet one day, and the teacher placed a large glossy picture of a red apple, with the letter 'A' in upper and lower case on an easel. We were told to write 'A' in our jotters, and the first one to complete the page would get a sweet. So I drew one huge 'A' over the whole page and ran out to the teacher's desk. She was amused enough to tell my mum, but the teacher was a woman of stern principle. No sweet.

We had multi-coloured pieces of plasticine to mould with, but poster paints were unknown. Our small jotters, less than half the size of standard ones, deemed suitable for the younger fry, had the rules for how to cross the road safely printed on the front cover. The bigger jotters that we graduated to had the times tables on the back cover, as well as the essential information of how many furlongs were in a mile, and how many ounces in a pound, pounds in a stone, stones in a hundredweight, and hundredweights in a ton. If I remember correctly, even pecks and bushels were mentioned.

We were told – in Primary One mark you – about God consisting of three persons, the Father, the Son and the Holy Ghost, just the way a shamrock has three parts. All those children in families with Irish connections had no difficulty identifying the shape of a shamrock. This seemed perfectly understandable, and I couldn't see why this was called a Mystery with a capital 'M'.

We started learning our Catechism at the age of five. This was a small paperback, about the size of an adult's palm, without pic-

tures and with a dull grey cover that did nothing to attract me to
its contents, and we rote learned its contents as we went through
school. It took a question and answer format.

'Who made you?'

'God made me.'

'Why did God make you?' and we would parrot back: 'God made
me to know Him, love Him and serve Him in this world and to be
happy with Him forever in the next.'

Just to help me to be good, I had a guardian angel all to myself.
We sang a hymn:

Guardian angel, from Heaven so bright,

watching beside me to keep me aright,

fold thy wings round me, oh guard me with love,

softly sing songs to me of Heaven above.

Naturally, when I went to Mass at Holy Cross in Dixon Avenue,
I wanted to keep a space beside me for my angel, but I was told
crossly not to be silly and move up.

They sang songs at Mass. I liked 'Hail Glorious St Patrick'. That
painted pictures in my mind of Erin's green valleys. 'Soul of My Saviour' seemed to be a great favourite. It had a sad tune, and it was all
about when you died and went to heaven, and what a good thing
that would be. But I didn't want to die. It was difficult to work out
who began the singing when the choir wasn't there. Could anyone
start up the singing, I wondered. I tried out an experiment. 'She'll be
coming round the mountain when she comes–' I began. They didn't
like that. Mum hushed me and looked around apologetically. It was
all very puzzling. Was that what came of not letting my guardian
angel sit beside me?

Then I fell ill with pneumonia. My angel must have been asleep,
or away somewhere. Kaolin poultices were applied to my chest.
For those too young to have heard of this form of torture, Boots
the chemists did a roaring trade in this grey, soft mud in a round
tin that had to be boiled, and then the hot contents smeared on
a piece of lint that was then stuck to your chest. Then there was
Thermogene, an orangey-pink fluffy material like candyfloss that

was intended to keep your chest warm. We all had liberty bodices – a kind of close fitting vest fastened down the front with studs – to keep the cold out too. It was rumoured that some children were fastened into theirs when winter came on and never had them taken off until the end of May. 'Ne'er cast a cloot till May be oot' was taken all too literally.

There was castor oil, the vilest taste known to human tongue. I don't even remember what ailment it was used for. It was probably like snake oil, believed to cure anything and everything.

My pneumonia was cured by the 'M&B' tablets the doctor prescribed – standing for May & Baker, the pharmaceutical firm's initials. No-one knew what it was, but we knew it wasn't penicillin. The bulk of such supplies as there were was reserved for the armed forces. It was only a few years ago, thanks to my good friend Tom Brown, who was a medical correspondent at some time in his life, that I discovered what those M&B tablets were: a particularly potent, and often dangerous drug, called Sulfanilamide. Even vets don't use it nowadays.

Regardless of May & Baker's kill or cure product, my mother was convinced it was her prayers to Our Lady, St Joseph and St Therese of Lisieux that had cured me of my pneumonia. Night after night she had said her Hail Marys, then she soaked a cloth in vinegar, wrung it out tightly and laid it on my fevered brow. It undoubtedly was comforting, even if I smelled like a fish supper. Jim and Joe made me laugh, saying they would shake salt on me and have me for their tea.

Govanhill was where I acquired the heritage of every Glaswegian tenement child. I, too, ran along the top of the high back court brick wall and dreeped fearfully to the ground. But I didn't do it very often. I just did it to show I could, and that was that. The boys seemed to derive endless enjoyment from showing off their derring-do. Girls would make mud pies in little metal cake tins bought at the hardware shop around the corner in Cathcart Road. One day one of my wee chums, Agnes, started crying her eyes out. As we busily dug up the earth with our spoons she lost balance and sat down in a puddle.

'What are you crying for?' I asked.

'My knickers are all wet and muddy, and my mammy will hit me,' she replied.

I assured her confidently my mother would not do that, so the obvious thing to do was to swap knickers. At night, when I was being undressed for bed, my mother's alarm baffled me.

'Why have you got these knickers? Where are yours? Where have you been? Now, you know I won't hit you. So tell the truth and shame the Devil.' That was her sure-fire way of getting you to own up to something.

She must have been particularly fearful because a short time before that, when I was playing alone in the back court, a man I had never seen before had tried to get me to take down my pants by offering me sweeties. He stood on the path in front of the back entrance to the close opposite ours in his brown raincoat, holding out boiled sweets wrapped in see-through paper in the palm of his hand and saying, 'Come in here and I'll give you sweeties.' I don't think I had yet been warned about taking sweeties from strange men, but some instinct told me to stay away from him. He seemed quite unlike the nice cheerful American soldiers with their chewing gum. A neighbour spotted him from her window two stairs up in the next close, and shouted at me, 'Stey there till Ah come doon. Don't go wi' that man.' He ran off. She came rushing towards me a moment later, in her wrap around floral pinny, gave me a reassuring cuddle and took me home. Nothing had happened to me, but nevertheless I was taken down to the police station for examination. My brothers were big lads for their age, and not minded to await the outcome of any judicial process. The neighbours said the man, who lived up the close opposite ours, fled to Australia the next day.

It seems to me remarkable that I remember so well an incident in which, fortunately, no harm befell me. I didn't know what he might do. It was pure instinct. I am certain I would not have gone with him. But if I had attempted to escape, and that neighbour had not been there to intervene, he could easily have caught up with me. Maybe such experiences are more traumatic than anyone realises at the time.

I actually felt more frightened when I found myself alone and in the dark in my big adventure. One summer afternoon I wandered off with some older children to look for the lucky middens in Strathbungo, a district nearby. People over there, I was assured, threw valuable things into their middens, just lying there for the taking. But when we got there the rubbish bins proved disappointingly empty of anything worthwhile. Manky and no doubt smelly from raking through the cinders and rotting food, we played hide and seek in those unknown streets until it was getting dark, and I stood alone for what seemed ages in an unfamiliar back court. I called out the names of the older girls, but to no avail. So I thought I had better get home. I hardly knew where I was going, but I could hear the trams going by in the distance. Having been up and down Cathcart Road often enough with my dad on his tram, I decided that was the way to go.

And yes, here were the shops I had been in with my mother. The fishmonger's with the picture of a blue mermaid on its white tiled wall at the side of the door. The ironmonger's shop where she had bought two little circular pieces of metal to screw onto the bottom of a pot, one inside, one outside, to cover where a hole had been burnt, when no new pots were to be had, every scrap of metal going to the war effort. I went on my way with more confidence. When I arrived at the foot of Govanhill Street there was my mother with a search party, stretched out from side to side of the road. Among them were some of the older girls I had been with at the lucky middens. I was grounded, so I played peever, kick the can and tig close to home.

Girls sat on the pavement crocheting blankets for their dolls' prams with wool unravelled from old cardigans. Or somebody would bring out a length of old washing rope, and we would play skipping games while we chanted some doggerel. A favourite ditty went:

There she goes, there she goes,
Like an elephant on her toes,
Look at her feet, she thinks she's neat,

Holes in her stockings and dirty feet.

Or we would go round and round, holding hands in a ring, singing:

Down in yonder meadow where the green grass grows
There [insert name of red faced girl in the middle of the ring] she
Bleaches all her clothes,
And she sang, she sang, she sang so sweet
That she sang [insert name of boy she likes] across the street...

Mothers sat on kitchen chairs, knitting or making fireside rugs out of small scraps of cloth. Boys ran after the lorries hurtling down the street, grabbing a hold of the tail end for a hurl and jumping off when they slowed for the corner. When planes flew overhead they claimed to recognise Spitfires. They would scare the wee ones, shouting, 'Jerry bomber coming!' Glasgow had its own Spitfire squadron, and one day when we were crossing George Square, in front of the City Chambers, there was a fighter plane on display that you could climb aboard. Mum let me join in the queue of excited wee boys. She thought she had a right tomboy for a daughter.

Dad brought home a toy white clay pipe and taught me to blow bubbles. You could make pretend money for playing at shops, by wrapping a bit of silver paper around a farthing, halfpenny, penny, threepenny bit or 'tanner' (sixpence) and rubbing it with a pencil to make the head show through. If we dressed up for Hallowe'en it was a matter of raiding our mother's belongings and teetering around in her shoes. My mother sadly lacked the items other girls could seize upon. All her life she only used Pond's Vanishing Cream and Coty face powder in a little gold compact. No lipstick, let alone mascara or eyeshadow.

My mother's idea of an outing was to visit one of her favourite churches. St John's in Portugal Street, where I was christened, and St Francis were nearby in the Gorbals, but best was when we crossed the suspension bridge over the Clyde to visit St Andrew's Cathedral. I would gaze around at the main altar, and the statues of saints on high up pedestals near the side altars. There was a life size sculpture of Jesus's body after being taken down from the cross, with Our Lady sorrowing at the death of her son. Mum knelt and said her prayers, and we'd leave after she had lit a candle. She had a habit of taking the tram to further flung parishes too. That way I got to be familiar with the geography of the city. She usually had flowers to leave for the Virgin Mary's altar, and preferably expensive ones like arum lilies.

She was also wont to visit Gorbals Library, an imposing red sandstone building with many steps up to climb. Not because she was in the least bookish. It was because she wanted to read the Glasgow Corporation Minutes to see if any houses were getting built, so that she could visit her councillor and pester him with her claim for a much-desired council house. The librarian would give me a picture book to look at while my mother pored over her big important papers.

I learned to read early because my brothers were avid readers of the *Hotspur*, *Rover* and *Wizard*, and they brought me home picture books from their visits to Woolworths in Union Street. I loved the sheer smell of a new book and looking at the pictures before I could read the words.

In my turn I first had a comic called *Playbox*, which hyphenated any words of more than two syllables. Then I graduated to the *Dandy*, *Beano* and *Film Fun*. That cinema-going age could sell a black and white comic to children who recognised characters like Arthur Askey, Gracie Fields and Old Mother Riley.

Considering it was wartime, I had a few beautifully illustrated books: an abridged *Alice in Wonderland* with a large white rabbit wearing a yellow checked waistcoat on the front cover, a Ladybird edition of *Cinderella* wearing the most gorgeous silver and white dress and a collection of nursery rhymes and stories with *Aladdin* in an exotic Chinese garden in the moonlight, lit by lanterns.

Lewis's Polytechnic in Argyle Street had a department in the basement, mostly given over to household goods, but there was a corner where you could get *McGlennon's Song Book*, which simply set out the words of popular hits. This came in handy when you could not quite make out the words being sung on the wireless. For years my brother Joe thought the words of a popular Irish song, about welcoming home an emigrant back to dear old Donegal, ran, 'shake hands with all the neighbours, and kiss the collie dog'. 'Colleens all' were the actual words.

The Colosseum department store in Jamaica Street was intriguing. When the assistant took the customer's money she would insert it, along with the bill, in a little cylindrical metal box that whizzed on an overhead line up to the cashier's office on the floor above, and she in turn would send the box back down with the receipt and the change. Older Glaswegians have fond memories of meeting 'dates' at Boots Corner, or alternatively the Shell, a reminder of wartime, in Central Station nearby. There was even a song, 'Meet me at the Shell, in the Central by yersel'.

Up Sauchiehall Street you could go to Trerons, Pettigrew & Stephens, or Copland & Lye, where my mother bought her nylon stockings when they went on sale after the war. They were only available one pair at a time per customer.

A trip to St Enoch Square always gave me the chance to see the steam trains arriving at the railway station that stood high above, and the curved stone wall that for years bore a dark blue metal hoarding that read, 'They come as a boon and a blessing to men, the Pickwick, the Owl, and the Waverley pen.' The railway station had a red painted machine that let you stamp out your name on a strip of metal for a penny.

Cooper's, just round the corner from St Enoch Square, was where our ration books were registered. It was a cut above the average grocer's. Such was Mum's only contact with middle class women. She observed their air of confidence as they made their demands or stated their complaints, and it was for that reason she wanted me to have the education she never had. She had no notion of any career for her daughter.

All this may sound like a woman of pretty formidable get up and go. When she was feeling well she was bouncing with energy, but the next day she could be totally inert. She suffered for many years from what was then diagnosed as neurasthenia, an illness characterised by lassitude, irritability, worry and hypochondria. Some medical historians believe it was the diagnostic predecessor of chronic fatigue syndrome. Before I went to school, and she would have been in her late 30s at the time, she was prescribed Phenobarbitone as a sedative. Freud believed the condition was a neurosis, rather than some kind of infection. Certainly, her GP once told me she was neurotic, when I asked about her obsessive behaviour like wanting the dishes washed all over again in case they weren't really clean. It was exasperating having to waste time carrying out such unnecessary instructions, and I must confess my impatience got the better of me. I feel sorry in retrospect that I didn't understand better what was the matter with my mother.

It was my brothers who really brought me up, because they had charge of me so much of the time. Yet they were normal boys, leading normal boys' lives, playing football in the street and getting a row from the polis. I believe, thinking back, I may have had more freedom to do as I liked than was normal for a girl at that time. My brothers would support me when my parents demurred. When I wanted help with something it was my brothers I turned to.

My dad worked long hours on the trams, and in my younger days, what with early bedtimes, I saw little of him. But I loved being allowed to stay up later than normal at the weekend to see my dad when he got home. He always came home as quickly as possible, no stopping off for a pint as far as he was concerned. And he always had my *Girl's Crystal* on a Friday night.

Chapter 3

'Oh, My Papa'

IN GOVANHILL STREET we lived quite far up the hill, but I could still hear the noise of the trams going by in Cathcart Road at night when I was in bed, and it had a comforting, lulling sound. Maybe that was my dad's tram, I often thought, and he would be home soon.

Less enjoyable was the sound of the midden men emptying the bins in the back courts in the dark at night. You could hear them shouting to each other as they banged and clattered the bins and trace their movements from the brick shelter where the bins were stored, through the close, and out to the street. Why they were doing this at night-time instead of in daylight I couldn't say. Maybe manpower shortages during the war meant they did longer shifts.

For most of his service Dad's tram was one of the datebox-shaped, open-ended type, but later he drove one of the magnificent Coronation trams that could reach 6omph. The tram seat backs could be slid through slits at the sides to let them face forwards or back, and this was the conductor's job every time the tram reached a terminus. Dad was on the trams for 25 years, before he moved to a clerical job with the Corporation, so we heard all the tramway jokes and folklore at first hand. The jokes were legion.

PASSENGER: 'Excuse me, conductress, does this tram go over the Jamaica Bridge?'
CONDUCTRESS: 'If it does Ah'll be the furst wan aff.'

The story went that one day two Polish officers had stepped aboard an overcrowded tram, and the conductress was shouting to the passengers standing squashed together on the lower deck, 'Come oan, get aff.' They remained standing on the lower deck, not understanding the patois, while other passengers got off. 'Youse tae,' she admonished them. 'Oh, thank you madam,' they replied, thinking she was exempting them from her ruling.

One Saturday night, when he was still in his first job as a conductor, the tram was heading for Garngad, a notoriously tough district, after the pubs had closed at half past nine. He saw a man stepping forward to board, swaying a little as he went. Two police constables, seeing an easy 'drunk and disorderly' arrest, made to lift him, but Dad said, 'OK, officer, I know this man. He's never given any trouble.' In truth Dad did not know him, he just felt the police were being unfair. The man sat down, saying, 'Thanks Jock,' and Dad thought no more about it.

Some weeks later, going through Garngad on a Sunday afternoon, he was on the top deck collecting fares when four young men started taking the mickey.

'He'll pey,' said the first.

'Naw, he's peyin',' said the second.

'Ah'm no peyin,' declared the third.

In those days all fares had to be collected between each station, half a mile apart. If you failed to do so, and an inspector (known to the staff as 'the Gestapo') climbed aboard and noted it and you would have your wages docked. Dad went through to the front of the tram, and called down to the driver: 'Hey, John. Stop the car. Some people upstairs areny payin' their fares.' A man's voice rose from amongst the upstairs passengers: 'Whit's the maitter?'

'These guys at the back areny payin' their fares,' my dad replied. All the passengers knew they would be held up until this carry-on was sorted out.

The man looked round, saying, 'Who'll no'?' It was the fellow he had rescued from a night in the cells. The four young men got into an immediate state of agitation. Each one dipped his hands in his pockets at once.

'Aw right, Joe, only kiddin'. Nae herm meant.'

'Who's that?' Dad asked one of the passengers and got the reply: 'Take a look at his breast pocket when ye're passin'. If ye annoy him, he takes aff yer ears. That's Joe the Bull.' Joe had three razors neatly lined up behind his hankie in his pocket.

Dad often had a long walk home from Langside Depot when he had driven in the last tram on his route. But one night a fellow driver told him he had worked out a plan. If you timed the final part of your tram's journey to the second, you could be within the timetable and still get into the depot in time for the last tram out going his way home. So Dad tried it out. After the last compulsory stop, he went full steam ahead and raced all the way to the depot. Thankfully no-one was standing at any of the request stops. As he shot through the huge entrance gates and brought his tram to a halt, a man tottered down the stairs from the top deck, saying to the conductress, 'That man's mad. Quite mad. I wanted to get off at Mount Florida! That's over a mile away, and I haven't been able to get out of my seat!'

During the war, Glasgow Corporation Transport Department wanted to train conductresses to be drivers, so as to release men for the armed forces. The conductress who worked on the same tram as Dad, for they always went in pairs, decided to take up this opportunity and set out for her first day's lesson. As she drove hesitantly along there was a horse and cart plodding very slowly along the tram lines right in front of her. 'Ring your bell', the instructor advised. She gingerly tapped the pedal with her foot, making an almost inaudible 'ping'. 'Do it again,' he said. Her second attempt was no more successful. 'Oh, hit the bloody thing!' he cried. So she drove forward, straight into the back of the cart. 'But you told me to hit it' she wailed in protest when he marked her down.

But before his tramway days he had quite a story to tell. At primary school in the Gorbals he had been an outstanding pupil, and his teacher entered him for the competitive examination for entry to St Aloysius' College, the fee paying top Catholic school for boys in Glasgow. Dad did very well and would have been awarded a scholarship. His teacher even offered to buy his schoolbooks for as many years as he attended. To no avail. He was the eldest of a family of five, and he had to leave school at the end of his elementary education at the age of 14, without benefiting from even a few years at the College. Poverty, no doubt, was the main reason, and many a family could hardly wait until their elder children could get out to work and bring home some much-needed income. Daniel, his father, would have been out of work for some time, having been blacklisted. But it is also true to say that Daniel was rather too fond of the whisky bottle. Our dad, as a consequence, had a lifelong contempt for alcohol, and felt great determination not to fail his own children in the same way.

Perhaps, though, his parents had some respect for education, because his young sister Sarah became a teacher, and later on a headmistress, a rare thing in the Gorbals at that time. She recounted telling her Primary One class in a Maryhill school one day about the Crucifixion. The crowning with thorns, pushed brutally down on Jesus' head. The long walk to Calvary, falling three times as He carried the heavy wooden cross. His holy mother sorrowfully meeting him. The nailing of His hands and feet to the cross…

'The bastards!' cried one tearful infant in the front row. 'The rotten bastards! Miss, I could get my big brothers and their pals to them.'

Dad's commitment to his family's welfare was total. He would work long shifts on the trams to bring home the maximum earnings possible. That was not a time when fathers considered their time at home could be more valuable than the money they earned. He had been on the dole for four years before getting the job on the trams, so there would have been a lot of spending to make up. When he got home he didn't just sink into his newspaper, although at the end of such a tiring day it would have been understandable if he did. He enjoyed getting us to solve puzzles, and one of the things he did was teach us respect for punctuation and grammar, but never to our boredom. He did it by telling stories. He would say 'I saw a barber's shop with this sign in the window:

WHAT DO YOU THINK
I'LL SHAVE YOU FOR NOTHING
AND GIVE YOU A DRINK'

We had to work out that there were two contradictory messages here, depending on the punctuation.

Then there was the story of the fishmonger who had a sign painted in his window in large white letters, saying 'FRESH FISH SOLD DAILY.' His pal advised him, 'You've got too many words. They're blocking the customers' view. What's the good of a big notice, if they can't see the fish? You don't need to say all that.' So he thought, 'I'll remove "sold" – after all, the customers know I'm selling, I'm not giving them away.' The next day he thought, 'I'll remove "daily", because it's not accurate. I'm closed on Sundays and Mondays.' Later on, he looked at his new notice and said to himself, 'No point in writing "fish". It's obvious I sell fish. It's a fishmonger's shop.' That left him with 'fresh', which didn't mean anything on its own, so he did without any notice at all.

When we moved to Pollok he worked with Joe in the garden, and we grew our own carrots, potatoes and strawberries. He supported Celtic but never went to matches. I don't remember him ever going out with mates, only with Mum occasionally to the cinema. When he was ill in Mearnskirk Hospital, where he died of heart failure in 1972, he chided me for extravagance when I brought him a couple of paperbacks. What did I think the public library was for? He liked his pipe, and his evening papers, the *Times*, the *News* and *Everybody's* magazine, and that was all he ever spent on himself.

Dad would regularly bring home a box of assorted cakes on Saturday afternoons. They were bought from a high class baker's shop that used to be in St Enoch's Square in the city centre, and I was always keen to see what was in the box. There would be iced French fancies, a fruit slice, a rhubarb pie, an almond slice and always one Eiffel Tower, a sponge that tapered from bottom to top, covered in some kind of sweet pink goo and coconut flakes. That was my favourite, but it happened to be Mum's favourite too. And that one was for Mum. So, I asked him to be sure to get two Eiffel Towers the next time he was in, but he never did. I got cross and refused any cake at all. I never got to the bottom of this. Did he just forget, having more on his mind than something as trivial as a choice of cake? Was he too shy to ask the snooty assistant for particular cakes, instead of leaving it to her to provide the standard selection? I even suspected that it was deliberate, one of his many small ways of giving Mum a special treat. Be that as it may, on the scale of paternal neglect, aren't I lucky that's the worst I can remember?

When, as I got older, I realised there were dads who drank their wages, abused and battered their wives and families, were so irresponsible their wives had to treat them like another child in the family, and generally made the lives of all around them a misery, it put my wee sponge cake into perspective. It has occurred to me to wonder why, if I was so keen on them, I didn't just make some myself. Simple. There were no such moulds in the shops, and in those days coconut flakes were far too exotic an item to expect to see on the grocer's shelves. Where we lived, anyway. Maybe such exotica were on sale in posh places like Hillhead and Kelvinside in the West End.

He was a member, as a young man, of the Knights of St Columba, an organisation of Catholic men founded in Glasgow in 1919 that does charitable work, but I know nothing about it as he would never reveal anything, having been sworn to secrecy. What they had that needed to be kept secret I have no idea. Did they, like the Masons, who are famous for being secretive, roll up their trouser legs, swear strange oaths and proffer funny handshakes? Somehow I doubt it. It would have been in the folklore, surely, just as it is with the Masons. Besides, I can't see my sensible, down-to-earth dad doing anything like that.

Dad did tell a story about a member in a state of annoyance at a meeting one night declaiming, 'I want to know. I demand to know. Why do we appoint officials–'

'To kick them, of course,' came a voice from the back of the hall.

That memory stood me in good stead when confronted in later life by people who were better at criticising than doing.

When he began working on the trams he joined the Catholic Transport Guild. I learned from a chap I met some years ago, Frank McMahon, whose own father was a tram driver in the same depot, that the main purpose of the Guild was to counter the influence of the Communists in the Transport and General Workers' Union.

'What particular issues did they disagree about?' I asked.

'Everything,' I was told.

I find this odd for two reasons. Dad never mentioned anything about Communism at home. Indeed, his membership of the Guild seemed to be about religious affairs, not jockeying for position in the union or battling over union policy. My brothers' recollection is that the Guild had more to do with being anti-atheism than anything else.

The second reason is that he took up issues of practical interest to fellow workers that I would have thought everyone could unite on, even if philosophically divided on how to run society. I know my dad often quoted 'Rerum Novarum', the papal encyclical calling for a just society, and deploring the excesses of capitalism, although hardly from a Marxist perspective. Frank McMahon distinctly recalled both our fathers regarding Ernest Bevin, who was no left-winger, as a hero.

The Guild staged Irish melodramas in a villa in Dixon Avenue to which I was dragged along. They were usually about innocent girls leaving a village in Ireland to go and work in some godless place over in Britain, and the misfortunes that befell them before they met a good Catholic boy and went back to regular attendance at Sunday Mass. There was a little magazine, about half A4 size, with a red cover, called *The Irish Messenger of the Sacred Heart*, which was sold along with all the Catholic Truth Society's abridged lives of the saints at the bookstall at the back of the church, and it always carried similar stories. Big cities like Glasgow were always seen as particular dens of iniquity.

The Guild organised annual visits to Carfin, and I was fascinated by my first sight of this reproduction of the grotto at Lourdes in our own Lanarkshire backyard, where there was a shop close by selling the kitschiest devotional items imaginable besides the normal stock of Rosary beads, that came in great variety, and statues of the saints. It had long stemmed wax roses with pink, red and yellow petals, and – oh, no, I don't believe it – bottles to hold holy water shaped like the statue of Our Lady of Lourdes, with a crown to signify her being Queen of Heaven forming the cap. I wasn't allowed to browse long. We had to get out and walk around the grotto in a group, saying the Rosary as we went. I had to concentrate and not think about the bottle cap, or I would burst into giggles.

Dad seems to have been pretty active in the Transport and General Workers' Union (T&G). He drew up a petition some time during the war years to allow the conductresses to wear either trousers or skirts as they pleased, and the men supported the women. Some idiot in the Transport Department had decreed that conductresses should not be allowed to wear trousers. Unladylike. Unseemly. Presumably he had never tried spending a shift on a cold winter's day, up and down the tram staircases that were open to the winds, in a skirt, with legs bare above the stocking tops getting frozen. This was decades before tights were invented. My brothers told me the Irish Catholic conductresses in Langside Depot regarded my dad as someone who would speak up for them. They didn't have T&G branch meetings, as far as I know, and no industrial action was envisaged. I expect some senior manager conceded the point. What was the sense in refusing? Conductresses safeguarded that bit more from the cold and bitter winds would be likely to take less time off sick.

When it was May Day, and T&G members from every tram depot marched along four abreast, my dad was amongst them. He had been involved in a campaign to seek permission for the staff to march in uniform, which was a convenience if you were working a shift that day. Besides, you travelled free if you were in uniform.

To get any job during the Depression was hard. Succeeding in getting on the trams was deemed nearly miraculous: people speculated that you must know somebody. Entrants had to pass a strict medical, which included having all your teeth. Why a full set of gnashers mattered, don't ask me. The better to bite the passengers with? Dad had been on the dole for four years, having been sacked from the Maypole Dairies where he had been a shop manager, and he failed the first medical on the grounds that he had a front tooth missing. The dole money in 1938 was 15s 3d for men, and it did not stretch, and never has, to cosmetic dentistry. The NHS was not to come into being until after the war. However, a local dentist told him that there was a way around it. If he got all his teeth extracted, and dentures fitted, that could be done without any payment as the powers-that-be would take it for granted that he must have a serious dental condition. And that is what my dad did to get a job. Every tooth in his head was extracted. He attended a second medical, where some sadistic clown tested his newly fitted dentures by asking him to eat his way through a Granny Smith apple, and it was agony, but he did it. My mother had a constant refrain that men were all selfish. This action alone contradicts that view, never mind so much else recorded in these pages. I never knew anyone more selfless than him.

My dad had no personal vanity about his looks. He was lean faced, and of wiry build, like James Cagney: not exactly handsome, but striking. But surely most people would have found the loss of their teeth, and the consequent effect on their appearance, too great a sacrifice to make? Then again, perhaps not. When the NHS started providing free dentistry, some people asked for teeth that were perfectly sound to be extracted, so that they could have a dazzling set of perfectly formed white teeth, which looked much better than the ones nature had given them All my life I saw my dad take out his dentures when he wanted to be really comfortable, giving him a gumsy look, handy for doing an impersonation of Popeye the Sailor for my amusement.

In his Maypole Dairy days, the directors ran a competition amongst the shop managers to see who could sell the most tea. Dad went down to the docks, boarded any ship he could, and took orders from the galley for enough tea to see them through weeks of ocean voyaging. His sales soared to a nationwide record high. This didn't save him from redundancy, though. When sales fell during the Depression, and the management wanted to cut staff, they didn't go by the usual formula, 'last in, first out'. Their policy was to get rid of their highest paid workers and keep on the cheaper, younger ones. So, if you worked hard and inventively like my dad, and earned more profit for the company, you got a half-crown raise, but every time you did that, the nearer you were to getting the push.

My dad told me about the time one of the staff arrived early one day before the shop had opened for business, and as he stood in the doorway he addressed a small tortoiseshell cat sitting there. 'Oh happy, oh happy wee cat,' he said. 'Oot playin' a' night, sleepin' a' day, an' never a care in the world.' The inspector had come up behind him. 'Well, if that's your attitude, you can join him. You're sacked.'

Another assistant was noticed one day doing tricks by sleight of hand to amuse his customer when giving change. 'What's your name?' the inspector asked. 'Campbell, sir,' the man replied. 'You're a liar, it's Walker,' came the reply. 'You're fired.'

The company had an annual dinner dance, known to the staff as the 'survivors' ball'. One year one of Dad's workmates called for a toast to 'absent friends', and he was sacked the following day.

Maypole Dairies have long since gone from the Glasgow scene, probably driven away by one or other of the expanding supermarket chains, and I like to hope that their employment policies led to their downfall. I'd hate to think that these malicious, heartless swine did well out of it. When I was growing up, and listening to my dad recounting these experiences, I thought, 'There ought to be laws preventing employers from doing that.'

Dad was born in 1900, and left school 14 years later when the First World War broke out. His first job was in a lawyer's office, doing clerical work, which – who knows – may have led to better things, but he had to leave because the pay was so low, and the family needed him to earn more.

He was lucky not to have been slightly older, so he missed the horrors of the Somme and Ypres in 1916. He volunteered before his 18th birthday, along with a bunch of his pals from the Gorbals. But not for patriotic reasons. Although born in Glasgow, he thought of himself as Irish, like thousands of other second generation Glaswegians. His reason was word had got round that those who volunteered would be demobbed sooner than those who waited to be called up. So along they all went to the recruitment office, where all his pals were allocated to the Highland Light Infantry, but Dad was told he was for the Gordon Highlanders. When he protested that he wanted to stay with his pals, the recruiting sergeant's answer was succinct. 'You're in the army now. You do what you're told.' Every one of his friends was killed in action.

After basic training was over he was sent to Belgium, where at five foot, seven inches he was the shortest in his Company. It was convenient for him that one of the officers didn't notice this, when he was detailed to join a party carrying heavy iron rails, to repair a railway track, on their shoulders. The rails were hefted onto the shoulders of the taller men, leaving him in the middle to march along bearing none of the weight at all.

They did notice his exceptionally good eyesight and sent him for training as a sniper. Snipers' life expectancy was zero. What he refused to do was train as an officer. Such was the loss of young officers at the front, the army was looking at under-educated young squaddies they would never normally consider. My dad did not want to be elevated above his mates. But then he was told he had to obey orders, and take the test, which consisted of writing an essay entitled, 'What I Think of the Army'. He did so in such frank terms they dropped the idea of promoting him but threatened him instead with court martial for insubordination. 'I was only following orders,' he replied. When he was demobbed an officer told him they had all had a good laugh in the mess at his forthright comments.

Posted to Germany, he was billeted with a family who wanted one thing explained to them. 'Tell me,' said the *hausfrau*, her brows knitting in puzzlement. 'I do not understand. You are an Irishman? In a Scottish regiment? Fighting for England?' His grandfather in

Kilrea wouldn't have seen it either. When his beloved grandson visited him on one of his leaves, wearing the Gordons uniform, he refused to allow him over the doorstep until he had gone back down the road to the railway station and changed into his civvies. The Easter Rising had been less than a couple of years before.

My dad had immense good luck to avoid death when he was in the front line in Belgium. One day four Companies were to be sent into battle one after another, and he was in Company C. Company A went up and recorded 40 per cent casualties. Company B, on the following day, recorded 25 per cent. For some reason the officers sent in Company D next, and then C was due to go up, but there was no reveille that morning. Instead all the men were called on parade. A general stood on a podium to address the squaddies all lined up and standing at ease on the square before him. As they were about to be informed, the Armistice had been signed the day before on the 11th of November.

'Men of the 51st Division...' he began. The men realised at once that the war must be over. They didn't hear the rest of his speech. They cheered themselves hoarse, then ran to their refreshment hut to celebrate. It was closed. The rule was it did not open until 12 o'clock. That was hours away. No matter. 'Rules was rules.' Not anymore. The men heaved up the wooden building, tipped it over on its side, and went for their beer. All the officers involved ended up being posted to another regiment, because they had not been able to keep order. My dad claimed, in recounting this story to us, that he went to the cathedral instead to pray thanksgiving for peace. An 18-year-old man, who had been just minutes away from the probability of serious wounding or death, and had newly re-alised he could eventually go home, uninjured and safe? I suspect this version was for our benefit, in case we were attracted to the demon drink.

His bad luck was to have to carry out mass burials in huge pits dug by the soldiers. He would never tell me any details, but to his dying day, although he faithfully bought a red poppy every No-vember, he maintained a hatred and contempt for the 1st Earl Haig that bore no comparison to any other public figure he ever mentioned. His point was simple. Anyone responsible for such squandering of men's lives should not have had his name attached to the annual memory of the fallen. Before my dad even joined up, as Alan Clark documented in *The Donkeys*: 'British commanders had shown their readiness to attack "regardless of loss", even if loss was to be the only result.'

Chapter 4

'Everything's Coming Up Roses'

NOWADAYS PEOPLE HOPE to win the lottery. My mum won a house. I don't mean she won it in a prize. No, in 1947 she was finally successful in getting the Corporation to allocate one to us. So it was goodbye private landlord and grim tenement. AND it was in the pleasant suburb of Knightswood, where every house had a well-tended front garden. The massive post-war house building programme had not yet begun, and these houses, built in the '20s or '30s, were much sought after.

Now we had a bathroom, not just an indoor toilet. The front door had a stained glass panel and led out to a sloping garden with a monkey puzzle and a holly tree; the back door opened onto a large garden that was all our own; and there were small air raid shelters still standing in every garden that were handy for storing tools.

At no stage, not for a second, did my parents ever share the nostalgic feelings that Adam McNaughton expressed in his song for the days of the room-and-kitchen and the single end. I never heard any song that celebrated getting people in their thousands away from the slums, away from the smells in the tenement stairwells, away from the sheer drabness of everything, and out to fresh air, to a space to call your own, and to a huge step up in the standard of living all round. Very few ever handed back their house keys to the Corporation factor and told them they wanted to go back to a slum tenement, complete with slum landlord.

February 1947 was the winter of the deepest snow anyone could remember since Victoria was on the throne. It was up to my head as I made my way to St Ninian's Primary School through the channel dug out by the householders along the pavement. The Forth & Clyde canal, just yards away from our front door, was solid, and although none of us possessed skates we slithered around on it. When spring came daffodils and irises grew wild – I had never seen any flowers except buttercups and daisies growing wild – along the bank, and a thick hedge of brambles and hawthorn had to be penetrated before you could reach the canal. The route to school was along the side of the canal. A creamy yellow painted wooden building, it stood near one of the locks, where there was a shop that sold cinnamon sticks to sweet-starved weans. I was introduced to my first poem at this school: Walter de la Mare's spine-tingling 'The Listeners':

'Is there anybody there?' said the Traveller,
　　Knocking on the moonlit door.

Christmas meant Santa would have to find me in my new house, and sure enough he did. So soon after the war there was not much to be had, but my great joy that year was a paintbox with 12 little blocks of paint, and a colouring-in book. My dad must have been tired when he came home from work, but he played Snakes and Ladders and Ludo with me. I had a wooden peerie and took ages to learn how to flick the thong so that it would spin properly and hit the ground and keep moving, instead of pathetically falling over. All the children created simple designs on their peeries with coloured chalks, so that our artistic efforts could be shown to good effect when the peerie spun round and round.

Collecting scraps was a favourite pastime for wee girls. We had crinoline ladies, cherubs and angels, baskets of flowers, fairies and elves and thatched country cottages decked out with hollyhocks and roses round the door. The older scraps from pre-war days were made of thicker paper and were more highly prized: being scarcer it was harder to form a complete set. The boys could keep their cigarette cards showing completely uninteresting stuff like football players, aeroplanes and battleships.

Christmas Day, and the clootie dumpling, made in an old pillowcase, fought for supremacy with Mum's Christmas cake. Dad put his foot in it the first time Mum made a fruit cake. Attempting a compliment, he said, 'This is every bit as good as the shops'.' Mum seethed visibly. The standard of wartime cakes in the shops was poor, which was why she had plucked up her courage to try making her own in the first place. Failure would have meant a waste of scarce foodstuffs. So, from then on we teased her every time she made a cake, saying judiciously as we munched, 'Well, it's maybe just as good as the shop cake this time. Could I have another slice to help me decide?'

The front page of the Christmas issue of the *Dandy* always showed Korky the Cat and his chums enjoying a perfectly spherical Christmas pudding, drawn with white icing dripping down its sides to resemble snow, and a sprig of holly on the top. I never saw such a thing in real life until I bought the mould in Lakeland. It may have taken me 50 years, but I was going to have a round Christmas pud someday.

Every year I 'helped' Mum make both the dumpling and the cake and put silver sixpences or 'wooden' threepenny bits into the dumpling. The cake was made to a recipe held in my mother's head, and every year she panicked about getting it right. It never failed. We ate large slices of it, cut across the entire width, on Christmas morning for breakfast. Those who had been fasting from midnight, as the Church ruled in those days that communicants must do, headed straight home from church and through the kitchen door for their piece of cake.

However, there was one snag. Knightswood was miles from my dad's tram depot and Holyrood, the secondary school my brothers attended. It meant changes of buses and long waits at bus stops in cold and wet weather. Then at last, in 1948, her dreams really came true. We were allocated one of the brand new houses in Pollok, built to a high standard of workmanship by the Corporation's own direct labour. There it stood, at the bottom of the hill, at the end of Braidcraft Road, in a terrace of six similarly pebble-dashed up-and-downstairs houses and sited much more conveniently. The house was still smelling of fresh paint. We excitedly trooped into view. At that time the post-war Labour Government had been three years in power, Clement Attlee was the Prime Minister, and if the Labour Party was united on one thing it was the absolute necessity of getting slum clearance and bomb damage tackled, and houses built that met modern standards. But I didn't know until I read a *Glasgow Evening Times* Times Past supplement just how lucky she was.

In 1946 an astonishing 172,320 out of 281,000 homes in the city were deemed unacceptable on standards of density. In Scotland as a whole, more than 400,000 homes were without toilets. In the cities, three houses out of every five had no bathroom. Homelessness was common. 170,000 young couples who had married during the war had no home of their own, and had to live, overcrowded, with relatives. Squatting was common and the need for housing so desperate it was suggested the homeless be housed in the Nissen huts that were used by the soldiers in wartime. Private landlords could put anything on the market and easily find a tenant. When, in July 1946, a house to let in Springburn, a tenement area in the north of the city, was advertised, no fewer than 937 applications were received.

The city authorities knew something had to be done, and fast. But even if 10,000 new houses were built every year, it would take until 1966 before everyone had a decent home of their own. The Corporation therefore decided to go for overspill to new towns, as well as building in the outer areas of the city.

How the new government managed such a vast programme of house building in so short a time, in those early post-war years, when our economy was in such a dire state we needed aid from the United States (that did not get paid off until Gordon Brown was Chancellor) deserves to be written up. Between the end of the war and March 1951 the number of houses completed (mostly in the public sector) was 865,000. At a time, too, when house building methods were much slower than now.

German prisoners of war had been deployed to build the roads and sewers for the new houses in Pollok. Local authorities all over the country had long waiting lists, caused by both bomb damage and the long-delayed slum clearance. Men who had fought in the war were determined things would change for the better. But it wasn't a case of longest waiting, first in queue. Or greatest need first.

Tenants were allotted houses not only according to need, but assessment by the local factor's office. Cleanliness, care of the property you were currently inhabiting as well as its fitments, rent and tenancy records were all checked. You only got a good house if you were considered not to require supervision. Identity cards were checked. References were sought. If graded for 'rehousing' – the lowest category – the tenant underwent regular supervision by the Health and Welfare Department until considered to have made sufficient improvement.

There were limitations that seem incredible today. There was only one electric socket in the kitchen. There was no such thing as central heating – indeed not until many decades later was it common – but we had a coal fire in the living room and in the bedroom immediately above. The hot water was supplied by a boiler at the back of the coal fire in the living room, so in summertime – when we had no need of a fire – there was no running hot water, and you had to carry pails full of hot water from the clothes boiler in the kitchen to the bathroom when you wanted a bath. Blankets and sheets were washed in the boiler, and everything else by hand with the aid of a washboard in the large Belfast kitchen sink, then wrung out by hand or mangled before hanging out on the clothesline or the overhead pulley in the kitchen. Each back garden had four green painted clothes poles.

The younger fry soon found new friends. We played on the banks of Levern Water, jumping in and out of the shallow water, and dug tunnels between the huge holes made along the riverbank by our dads and big brothers in their search for good, crumbly earth to improve upon the heavy clay soil in our gardens. The earth was carted in barrows 'borrowed' from the building site across the road, where yet more houses were going up. There were metal struts crisscrossing underneath the footbridge, that we held onto one hand at a time, feet dangling above the water, as we crossed to the riverbank opposite. Tarzan had nothing on us. One time when my pals and I were playing rounders a boy who lived round the corner from me jumped up and grabbed our ball. As he taunted us, refusing to give it back, he unwisely stood with his back to the riverbank. I pushed him in with all my might, and then ran like hell back home, because he was bigger than me and would soon catch up. I made it through my front door with him just a few feet behind, sopping wet and in a rage. Still, he never annoyed us again.

The houses under construction made an adventure playground. When the workers went away at night we clambered up into the half-built houses, jumping from joist to joist across floors that were not yet laid. We wandered past the construction site to the Blue-bell Woods, where the flowers were so abundant it was difficult to avoid tramping on them. When we got home we rinsed out any empty glass milk bottles we could lay our hands on and pressed them into service as vases. We were taught at school how to paint designs on them with lacquer paint bought in little pots from Wool-worths. The Co-operative Dairy's milk bottle neck was so narrow you could only get half a dozen stems inserted. But it had to do. Nobody had money to buy such a luxury as a vase, and in any case there were few if any to be had in the shops.

Crookston Castle lay atop a nearby hill and provided further opportunity for our imaginations to run riot. There was anoth-er wood downhill from the castle, with low hanging branches, so dense we could make secret hideaways by pulling branches togeth-er, or we would lie atop overhanging branches to ambush those passing below. We played Robin Hood, cops and robbers, cowboys and Indians, spies and secret agents – and that was just the girls. During the school summer holidays we stayed out until the setting sun warned us that maybe it was time to get home. If you got home in good time there was a well-fired roll to be had from the baker's van, spread liberally with butter, and a cool drink of milk from the larder. No-one had a fridge. The larder was fitted with wooden ve-getable drawers, which made first class toboggans for us to slide down the hill when winter's snow came, but they performed well on grassy slopes in summertime too.

There being no pavements locally, so as to prevent my long white satin dress from getting dirty my brother Joe carried me through the mud to Old Pollok, where I could progress on foot to my First Holy Communion in St Robert's Church in Househillwood. Mum had made the dress, and a blue velvet cloak to keep me warm. At our confirmation the following year we all sang, 'Fai–aith of Our Fa–a–the–ers living still, in spite of dungeon, fire and sword,' belting it out, while birds flew in and out of the open windows. I don't remember why I chose 'Veronica' for my confirmation name. I'd probably been reading about her offering Jesus her kerchief to mop his brow as He trudged to Calvary, and on receiving it back found His face imprinted on it.

But before any of that there was First Confession. We were told to remember if we had been naughty, or told lies, and how many times. In the Confessional you would kneel down and begin, 'Bless me Father, for I have sinned. This is my First Confession.' The priest would hear your list of transgressions, and give you a penance, such as saying three Hail Marys. My pal Mora Carty entered the Confessional, knelt down, made the sign of the cross, recited the opening words she had been taught, then told the priest she had committed adultery. He was clearly very concerned.

'What did you do, my child?' he asked. 'What makes you think you committed adultery?'

'Well, you see Father,' replied Mora, 'I got my dress all muddy when I was out playing.'

Baffled, the priest pressed her further. 'But why did you say adultery?'

Mora answered, 'Well, you know how it says on the salt packet, "This salt has not been adulterated?" I asked my dad what that meant, and he said it meant it had not been made dirty.'

My brother Joe invented a game, as we sat at the back of the church at Sunday Mass when the new St Conval's chapel was built much closer to home. The newly appointed parish priest was understandably somewhat obsessed with getting the loan paid off. Every sermon he gave, on no matter what subject, eventually turned to the church building fund. Joe and I would guess the number of steps it would take him to get from, say, the sin of gluttony to the building fund. Step One: gluttony is selfish when others are without food and starving for want of the sustenance you are scoffing so carelessly. Step Two: it is also bad because you should treat the body God gave you with respect. Three: it wastes money. Four: this money could be better spent on – guess what?

The Corporation had laid brick paths outside our back doors: quite fashionable nowadays, but we all said that was for the peasants, and what we wanted was the modernity of smooth concrete. Our next door neighbour, Mr Torrance, turned out very handily to be a pavier to trade, and he set to, one summer's day, carefully smoothing wet cement along the paths. My kitten, the well named Frisky, had to be kept out of the way. He had only recently helped himself to one of Mrs Torrance's haddock fillets that she had left temptingly within reach through her open kitchen window. 'If cats had consciences,' she said, 'his would be as black as his coat.' Now he was locked away safely, I thought, in my bedroom upstairs, but I forgot about the open window. As I stood in the garden, hanging out a washing, I witnessed Frisky's bid for freedom. He leapt in a graceful arc from the windowsill. He landed somewhat less gracefully on Mr T's bare back, scrabbling to gain his balance and digging in with his claws. Then he was off again, running all the way along the wet cement, a trail of paw prints in evidence against him. I had never heard such effing and blinding.

Each classroom in St Conval's had a coal fired stove and in winter we were asked to bring in a lump of coal, wrapped up in newspaper, every day. Winters then were so cold that chilblains were painfully commonplace, and smog was common when everyone had coal fires. A black cloud of smoke used to hang over Glasgow.

My mother bought – to my embarrassment – brown leather gaiters to keep my legs warm. I would take them off as soon as I was out of sight, hidden by our neighbour's tall hedge, and shove them in my schoolbag. This exposed me even more to the cold, as the gaiters were fastened with tiny awkward buttons from knee to ankle. I survived.

Mr Savage was one of the few male teachers around. Tall, thin, with balding grey hair, he encouraged my efforts at writing stories, but was sadly unconvinced that a plausible reason for a wooden boat sinking was a shark biting a hole out of the hull. I wrote my stories in a small cash book that Joe brought from work, no other paper being available.

Schonell's *Spelling Book* must be remembered by generations of children, and not always with affection. We learned to spell words by rote from the words listed in increasing order of difficulty, ending with 'antidisestablishmentarianism.' The inspector came one day, and Mr Savage asked me to come out to the front of the class and read out the words to be spelled by my fellow pupils. I can only imagine his annoyance and embarrassment when I refused. I asked if I could whisper to him, and then told him it was a better idea to get Mary Kelly to read out the words, because she was hopeless at spelling, and that way the inspector wouldn't know that anyone in the class was so bad at it. 'Just do what I ask, will you?' he whispered back. Then he shook his head and shared a smile with the inspector while I did what I was told.

I joined the ballet class at the community centre down at House-hillwood Roundabout and pirouetted around the house in my pink satin pumps, practising for my invisibly minor role in the *Dance of the Sugar Plum Fairy*. Nearby was the library, and I longed for the day when I would be granted an adult ticket and get more books. This was where I discovered Frank Richards' Greyfriars School stories about Harry Wharton and Billy Bunter, and Rider Haggard's adventures. I also read my mother's magazines: *The People's Friend*, *Red Letter*, *Red Star*, *Woman* and *Woman's Own*. I was fascinated by the problem pages. An awful lot of letters seemed to be from young women who had 'yielded' to their boyfriends and were now worried about the consequences. What was that all about? And why, I asked Mum, did people say the girl had behaved badly when she said it wasn't her fault? Mum just said, 'I'll tell you when you're older.' How often children are frustrated by that reply.

A favourite game when we weren't allowed to wander off was 'ghost in the garden', that I played with my neighbouring chums,

Joyce and Effie. By dint of wrapping yourself in a white sheet you could scare the life out of the more nervous children. My chums went to Shawlands Academy, the 'Proddy' (non-denominational) school but we never discussed religion, other than to muse on why the Protestants said, 'Our Father WHICH art in Heaven', and the Catholics said 'WHO'. I argued the Catholics won that one on grounds of correct grammar. You wouldn't say, 'Our mother, which is in the kitchen,' would you? Effie's dad, overhearing our conversation, told us it was just a matter of what people were used to, and went indoors singing, 'You like tomaytoes, and I like tomahtoes...' Joyce's parents talked about their 'garding', and I could not persuade them that 'garden' was the proper word. I seem to have been a pedant even then.

Large bats flew in from the woods at night, and they were a bit scary, especially if you were told they would suck your blood if they got into your bedroom. When a large bird flew overhead the older children told the wee ones they could carry away a sheep, and if they could do that, they could pick them up too, and the wee ones would run screaming to their mothers.

We had to be careful not to tramp on the seed beds or the plants that our dads were carefully cultivating. All the tenants where we lived planted privet hedges from cuttings and grew flowers and vegetables from seed. Mum and I walked around on a summer night, observing what other people had been doing in their own patches. We grew our own strawberries, carrots, lettuces and potatoes, and for the first time in my life I saw lupins, snapdragons, sweet peas, marigolds and primroses. In our own garden! A rambling rose grew up our back wall, and I could cut as many as I liked for display indoors. It was soon after the war, and fresh produce at your own back door would have been part of the joy of the move to a new house. It had been impossible to grow anything in the back courts of the tenements.

There was no vandalism or graffiti in Pollok then. Whatever the gangs of those days did to amuse themselves, when they weren't fighting each other with bicycle chains and knuckledusters, it wasn't trashing other people's houses. Any would-be vandals knew they would be lynched if they laid waste to any empty house in that time of desperate shortage. Although drunkenness was common, drug-taking was completely unknown.

Our new house had three bedrooms, a living room, kitchen and bathroom. New furniture had therefore to be bought to fill all this space. Twin beds, as seen in the films, seemed infinitely smarter than doubles. A bedside cabinet was an unfamiliar luxury. How I loved going into town to buy a bedside lamp, and never having to get out of bed to turn out the light when I was too sleepy to read any longer. My dad delighted in his new smoker's armchair, with wooden magazine racks down the sides and a small metal ashtray that swung out and in. Mum got her long-awaited hide sofa. No more horrible Rexine. On the new sideboard, matching the dining table and chairs, sat a wooden clock with Westminster chimes. We could only afford linoleum for the floors, cold to put bare feet on when you got out of bed on a winter's day. We got a wireless, a very swish item shaped in a semi-circle, not the usual rectangular box. We ran up and down the wavebands, finding exotic stations like Hilversum and Athlone. My mother frequently tuned in to Radio Eireann, the Irish commercial station, so we heard jingles for Donnelly's sausages. On Fridays I wished I was eating anybody's sausages, instead of white fish poached in milk. Yeugh! Catholics were required not to eat meat on Fridays. But why that got translated by many a Catholic mother into eating fish cooked in the most unappetising way ever devised remains a mystery.

Radio Luxembourg was my brothers' favourite, especially for the Top 20 hits of the week. It constantly advertised Silvikrin shampoo, Gibbs Dentifrice – which came in little round blue, red or green tins – and H Samuel's Ever-Right Watches.

I would ask my mother to call me in when *Dick Barton, Special Agent* was on the wireless. It had a great theme tune, 'The Devil's Galop', and Dick and Snowy had exciting adventures that were not to be missed. But who, in my generation, could forget *Much Binding in the Marsh*, the *Billy Cotton Band Show*, Jimmy Edwards in *The Glums*, *Two-Way Family Favourites* (a request programme for people at home and away in the forces), *The McFlannels* (Helen W

Pryde's chronicle of a Glasgow family and their neighbours) with its 'The Glasgow Highlanders' theme tune, *Children's Hour* with 'Down at the Mains' and 'Tammy Troot', the plays on *Saturday Night Theatre*, Wilfred Pickles' *Have a Go* show, and the Palm Court Orchestra playing light classics.

We got our home decoration ideas from the Modern Homes Exhibition at the Kelvin Hall, where people trooped in their thousands to see the latest in furniture and gadgets. One year in the early 1950s, the height of fashion was to have one wall papered in contrast to the rest of the room. One of our neighbours thought, as she looked in our window as she passed by, that we must be incredibly bone idle as we had started wallpapering months ago and had still not got round to finishing the job.

One Christmas when I was about 12 or 13 was the best of all because, my mother being unwell, I had the job of going into town to buy all the items on a lengthy festive shopping list, but most importantly, I had to visit first the poulterers near the Saltmarket to buy the chicken for the Christmas dinner. Chicken was an exceptional treat, and you had to choose your bird carefully, comparing their plumpness as they hung on hooks overhead. Having completed that task, and hoping Mum would approve my choice, I then went to Woolworths to buy baubles for the tree, paper chains, wrapping paper for the prezzies I intended to give (my parents considering any such purchase a waste of money when there was perfectly good brown wrapping paper in the sideboard cupboard) and a calendar of Scottish scenery to send to Jim in America. Joe was detailed to get the sherry, and he brought back one of the first bottles of Cyprus sherry to reach our shores. Our parents were dubious about this, but their drinking experience was so limited they couldn't have told a decent sherry from cough mixture. It was poured into our newly acquired gold-rimmed little carafe with matching glasses – oh, the elegance!

Our Hogmanays followed one age-old tradition. We cleaned out the house from top to bottom, emptying the grate, and leaving not a speck in the ashtray. I still feel I have to do that and feel out of sorts if I don't. I've put out rubbish at ten to midnight, after trying to ignore it sitting there and telling myself it could perfectly well wait until morning. Big Ben tolling the 12 bongs did not bring any immediate cheer. Before being allowed to touch a drop of any drink, or eat any shortbread or cake, we had to kneel down and say the Rosary. That takes a long time, bare knees on the lino floor, eyeing the goodies wistfully.

And then we would party at last. We'd sing 'Harbour Lights', 'Slow Boat to China', 'I Wonder Who's Kissing Her Now?', 'Me and My Shadow' and 'Chattanooga Choo Choo'. Someone ridiculously old would sing 'Too Young'. Some pious soul would offer 'Ave Maria' or 'Panis Angelicus'. Then there were the songs of Ireland that Mum would sing, 'Galway Bay', or 'Danny Boy', which still makes me fight back the tears. Joe was so un-tuned into popular music he couldn't tell 'Sonny Boy' from 'Danny Boy'. Jim gave me my first taste of classical music, singing 'Take a Pair of Sparkling Eyes' and 'Now Your Days of Philandering are Over'. My dad only ever sang one song at family parties, a doleful Irish emigrant's farewell, 'The Boat Leaves the Harbour Tomorrow', with the exception that at Christmas he would sing his favourite carol, 'See Amid the Winter Snow'. He hated 'The Mountains of Mourne'. He felt it made the Irish look stupid, and how right he was.

Although proud of their Irish ancestry my parents would not let Irish rebel songs be sung in the house, and certainly not in retaliation to the young man next door playing 'The Cry was No Surrender'. My parents felt those days were dead and gone. Ireland had won its freedom. No point harping on about it.

Chapter 5

'We're All Going on a Summer Holiday'

MUM DEPLORED THE way many landladies in the Clyde coast resorts who let out rooms to holiday makers required their guests
to leave immediately after breakfast, rain or no rain. No matter if
all they wanted to do was play a game of draughts, or have a long
lie, or read a book. Why so inhospitable? If you don't like people
hanging around your house then maybe you should find another
occupation. So Mum was determined, as soon as we could afford
it, to have a holiday in a boarding house where you had freedom to
come and go as you wished.

We prayed for sunshine when we took the steam train from
Central Station or St Enoch's to Largs or Saltcoats, or boarded a
steamer at Gourock for Dunoon, or Wemyss Bay for Rothesay. If
our prayers were not answered, we would soon be joining the de-
jected families cowering on the wooden seats in the shelters along
the seafront while the rain lashed them remorselessly and thinking
we may as well take a dip in the sea as we couldn't get any wetter.
Or we'd sit in wet raincoats, surrounded by women with rainmates
covering their perms, umbrellas dripping down the back of our
chairs, spinning out a tea and bun in a café. Even when the weather was good enough to take out a rowing boat, or have some fun
splashing about in the lido, you couldn't spend all that much time
larking about in the water. Not in the temperature of our northern
waters. We must have been a hardy lot to go in at all. We would
come back up the shingle beach, chittering with the cold, and get a
hot tea from the thermos flask.

The first boarding house we ever stayed in was the Mount Carmel in Kirn, a small, quiet resort on the River Clyde. It was owned and run by a thin little woman who dressed so drably everyone on first acquaintance thought she must be the skivvy. She would stand at the door to welcome you in, wearing a high necked, long sleeved, black rayon dress that had seen better days, her only jewellery a cameo locket on a silver chain, thick woollen stockings and scuffed flat shoes, her greying hair tied back in a bun that was always losing anchor.

This incredibly large house was a paradise for children, offering many a nook and cranny to explore. Each bed had a patchwork quilt and in your bedroom there was a marble topped dresser on which stood a rose patterned ewer of water and matching bowl to wash in, a peculiarity I revelled in until she got washbasins fitted. En suites were unknown then. When you wanted a bath, you kept your eyes open for when the bathroom down the corridor fell vacant and raced to get there with your towel and soap before anyone else beat you to it. The lounge had bumphly armchairs covered in chintz, and bookcases full of magazines and yearbooks from the Edwardian era. I was fascinated with the ads for hats and floor length dresses as worn by the Suffragettes. And best of all, a huge back garden filled with bushes and trees and foxgloves allowed me to disappear.

At every mealtime we sat down in rows at long tables – there were no such things as separate tables – so the conversation flowed. They were hearty meals. At high tea, to follow after the hot main course or generous ham salad, there were three-tiered floral plates filled with dainty little triangular sandwiches on the bottom layer, a variety of scones on the middle one and fancy cakes on the top. It was bad manners to pick up a cake before you had eaten both a sandwich and a dreary scone. So I chewed my way through my scone if I could not get away with putting it in my pocket, while keeping my eye on the cakes. Not that you could reach for whatever cake took your fancy. Oh no. Properly brought up children took the cake that was nearest. If an empire biscuit, that dry and boring invention that I felt hardly qualified as a cake, happened to be the closest one I accepted my fate. I would sit wondering if anyone actually liked these things, and deliberately bought them. Never mind, with any luck I'd get an Eiffel Tower or a Fly Cemetery to-morrow. Or, come to think of it, I could nip in early and turn the plate in an advantageous direction.

Kirn had a rundown little café opposite the pier, but it had an elderly fruit machine, so old it hardly had a lick of paint left on it. One day I had a return on my small daily investment, and out poured a great heap of tokens. Very little cash, unfortunately. Yet here was the impossible dream: a knickerbocker glory every day, not only for me, but anyone who cared to join me.

The lending library facing the pier – a shop that charged a small fee for the loan of books – was much more to my taste. I could get there all the books I wanted for the whole holiday. The owner took an interest in my reading and introduced me to PG Wodehouse's novels. In between was the shop specialising in needlework para-phernalia. I never mastered crochet, but I enjoyed watching Molly, my mother's friend, who regularly stayed at the Mount Carmel. She would sit on a deck chair in the front garden lawn, her deft fingers quickly creating beautiful table runners and cheval sets, adorned with purple, lavender and yellow pansies or shell-pink roses, out of a few skeins of silk from that shop. She made them for her church bazaar or any good cause she wanted to support, and her annual fortnight's holiday from some boring job, when she could get busy with her hooks for hours, seemed to be all she wanted from life.

My parents had not found the Mount Carmel by looking at ad-vertisements but had become familiar with nearby Kirn on earlier trips to Dunoon. My mother had enjoyed a few convalescent short breaks in Dunoon in a place run by the Co-op, which used to pro-vide that service to members who needed some rest and recupera-tion. It couldn't have been much of a rest, considering she had to take me with her. One day when she was getting an afternoon nap, the matron handed me the first jigsaw I had ever seen. This was intriguing. It had quite a lot of small pieces, but I got the hang of it and completed it. The matron was amazed and told me I was a clever girl. No-one had ever said that to me before.

Mum would take daily walks from Kirn around the Holy Loch

to the small waterside villages of Hunters Quay, Sandbank and Ardnadam, and occasionally if the rain stayed off take the bus to Kilmun, six and a half miles from Dunoon, and walk back at least some of the way. Now, anyone might imagine these walks of upwards of two miles were taken in sensible, flat heeled shoes, no. Mum never possessed a pair of flatties in her life, considering them too unbecoming. If I walked such distances in peerie heels I'd be ready for the knacker's yard, never mind needing convalescence.

Many years later, in 1960, the Americans sited their Polaris submarine base on the Holy Loch. An ad appeared in the property pages for a Victorian sandstone villa sited on the loch shore, described as 'suitable for a brothel keeper or Russian spy'.

Everyone of a certain age remembers well the steamers that sailed 'doon the watter' up and down the River Clyde. Children – and the not so young – liked to identify, from the colour and the number of the funnels, which one was sailing into view before it came close enough to read its name on the bow. I would get on at Kirn, and sail to Rothesay where I would be met at the pier by my pal Mora Carty and her parents and brothers, who always stayed in a ground floor flat they regularly rented for a whole month, the lucky devils, right next to the municipal baths. On wet days we were never out of the baths, and on good days we took out a rowing boat. The River Clyde resorts all had umpteen boat hirers plying their trade, their boats sitting side by side on the shingle beach. Most of their customers were never in a boat from one summer to the next, and few could swim. This brings back memories of the year my brother Joe took the family out in a small motorboat, not realising the water was less deep than on the previous occasion, and decided to go round the Gantocks, a scatter of rocks close to Dunoon's west bay. He carefully gave the nearest rock a 20 yard berth, but then we heard the bottom scrape on another rock. The sea was heaving as we tried to get afloat again. We were overloaded, having cheerfully ignored the warning notice saying 'maximum four passengers', and water was slopping in. Joe was more worried than he let on. But hooray for the steamers. As one of them sailed out from the nearby pier its wash floated us free. When back on dry land we saw the tide go out some six hours later, and took in the long, jagged row of rocks that we had been stuck on. Gulp!

But I also loved the red single decker Western SMT buses, with their 'classic' design, that plied their trade throughout Argyllshire. Call me a sentimentalist, but a modern wide fronted panoramic windowed bus just isn't the same. You could catch a bus at a stance close to Dunoon Pier to go anywhere along the coastline or inland, and that was a treat in itself. In the early '50s the bus operators offered a variety of tours around the lochs, stopping for a while in some hostelry in Glendaruel or Arrochar for entertainment and a 'refreshment'. Widespread car ownership seems to have killed off the bus run trade, yet it had the advantage of fun and companionship as well as the stunning scenery, and only the bus driver needed to keep his eye on the road. The unfortunate driver of the family car doesn't get to see the eagle soaring, or the pretty flowers at the wayside, or the heather on the hills.

In my early teen years, the bit where we got to the hostelry was excruciating to me. Too old to play, and too young to enjoy adult company, I would bring a book and only get up to dance when nagged by my parents to join in a Pride of Erin or a Gay Gordons. Donald Dewar once told me that, at a similar age, on a cruise with his parents, he avoided socialising by hiding in one of the lifeboats.

My mother would always entertain the company with a song or two. I can see her now, standing by the piano, in her new pink paisley-patterned summer dress I had persuaded her to buy at C&A, tapping out her cigarette before telling the pianist the key, and launching into favourites like 'Kathleen' or 'Sweet Vale of Avoca'. She was always asked for an encore.

Everyone was supposed to have their party piece to contribute. She and Dad had a pal called Eddie from the east end of Glasgow, who always told the same dreadful jokes when it was his turn.

'A man goes into a pet shop in Dublin, and asks "How much for the brown parrot in the window?"

'The shopkeeper answers, "It's not a parrot, it's a night owl."

'Customer: "I never asked you how old it was, just its price."'

Eddie took it upon himself to object when he noticed me reading one of Peter Cheyney's mystery, murder and mayhem novels as I sat, engrossed in the adventures of Lemmy Caution, the hero, on a deck chair in Mount Carmel's garden. He didn't like me reading Leslie Charteris's Saint novels either. Yes, the stories that provided family entertainment on TV years later, with Roger Moore in the title role. He told my parents my choice of book wasn't suitable for a girl of my tender and innocent age, on account of there being an illustration of a glamorous woman in a low cut frock on the front cover, but my brothers came to my rescue. They assured Mum and Dad the books were completely harmless. They would have done so anyway. They had a liberal view not shared by my parents. I'm not so sure they were totally harmless. I used to ponder how I could get myself into adventures like The Saint regularly managed to do. Perhaps if I followed a suspicious looking character...? I actually did one day, when coming home from school on the Underground. The man sitting opposite looked shifty. I followed him off the train, down the street, ready to turn aside and look at a shop window if he should turn around, keeping my distance successfully until he disappeared into – a church. Oh, well.

We didn't go to seaside shows. To be strictly accurate, we once went to some show in the Pavilion in Dunoon, but my parents were so shocked by the comic's patter they got up and left immediately, pressing their way past people's toes along the row of seats. I re-member it clearly. The comic was doing a female impersonation, and was fending off a would-be suitor, who, after successfully grab-bing hold of her around the waist after a hilarious chase around the stage, counted down the huge buttons on her blouse, saying 'Eeny, meeny, miny, mo–' swiftly followed by the comic interject-ing, 'that's the furthest you can go.'

'That's disgusting,' my mum said as she stalked out, with me scurrying after and hoping no-one knew me.

Our holiday ambitions grew, and we took a plane to the Isle of Man. Holiday flights were so rare then that photographers would stand at the foot of the stairs snapping people as they came down off the aircraft and give them a card to let them know where they could pick up their photo at a very reasonable price.

I had outgrown my knitted woollen swimsuit and packed my first adult costume. It had taken me hours to find it in the shops, looking for something that was grown up but not glamour girl. I used to imagine that the salesgirls were secretly laughing at me, as I tried on swimsuits and bras. In some swimsuits the cups were boned to create the impression of a bust where little or none existed but would have deceived no-one of average vision. Even worse, there were padded bras with circular stitching that made your breasts look like cones jutting out. Bikinis were out of the question. I would look ridiculous. Often, then, swimsuits would be worn by women who never got them wet. They simply wanted to show off their figures and their tan if they had one. I had no such ambitions. I wanted only to hide away somewhere. My teenage years were in the '50s, when Marilyn Monroe and Jayne Mansfield made flat-chested me feel even more reluctant to be seen. So, I sat on the beach, wishing it was time for tea, hunched over an Aldous Huxley novel that I only admitted to myself was pretty hard going, but promising myself a PG Wodehouse when I finished it.

A beauty competition was being held, and my dad, convinced no-one could hold a candle to his darling daughter, urged me to enter. The prize money was a small fortune that he thought I could gain for myself. But a 34A bust and skinny legs? No chance. So, I refused point blank. My refusal had nothing to do with feminism. At that stage I did not have a feminist thought in my head. It was just realism about my chances. Even if I had met the criteria, I knew I could never sashay across the stage in the approved manner. Dad seemed to me too innocent to realise that the judges – and the crowd – were mainly interested in the contestants' vital statistics, and I could not attempt to explain. How could anyone miss it? The contestants had their pictures in the local paper, with their bust, waist and hip measurements set out in the captions below. They were all 'raven haired' (never merely black), blonde or redheads. None had mousey brown hair. Nothing else about them was deemed worthy of note. It had not yet occurred to such hopefuls to claim an interest in world peace or helping starving children. I had been at a few dances at St Mungo's Academy, a boys' school, where one youth boasted he never asked a girl to dance who was less than a 36C. How could he tell, I wondered. Yet while I felt contempt for the arrogant brat, who was good looking and boy, did he know it, the beauty competition audience probably had more in common with him than with my dad. A few years later Twiggy came along, but too late to help with my teenage angst.

Dad won a competition, though. The local weekly newspaper boosted its sales by assembling crowds for photographs, with the intention of picking out one individual for a prize. He looked away to the side, puffing his pipe, as if he had little or no interest in what was going on. His prize was free entry to all that was going on that week. Not that he was interested – my brothers and I got the benefit. Best of all there was a huge ballroom where The Squadronaires – a big band formed by RAF men – played all the popular dance tunes. Johnny Dankworth and Cleo Laine also entertained. By this time, I was interested in dancing. My brother Joe had taught me to do the waltz, quickstep, foxtrot and jive, and I had an illicit shandy while I sat infatuated by the crooner singing 'Night and Day'.

Then when I turned 19 I was considered old enough by my parents to be allowed to go on holiday without them. Not abroad, though. That was out of the question. Anywhere in Ireland was considered suitable by my parents. Irish Catholic boys, they said, would be 'respectful'. That was their way of saying not likely to Go Too Far. Little did they know. So, my old school chum Mora Carty and I set off by train and steamer for Portstewart in Northern Ireland. Unlike Glasgow, where there was a variety of glamorous ballrooms to choose from, there was only a large, charmless hut near the beach in the larger resort of Portrush, further along the coast. But first things first – what were the boys like? We were soon to find out. The band was playing that summer's hit tune, Bobby Darin's 'Dream Lover' as we entered, and the singer was giving it laldy. This was promising. We danced away, the night wore on, we found ourselves congenial company.

It should be mentioned that, as Glaswegians, we were accustomed to paying no attention at all when our national anthem was played at the end of any entertainment. The cinemas used to play it at the end of a night's performance but gave it up as everyone made for the exits to get into the bus queue. But this was Northern Ireland. The weekend before the 12th of July. So, as we sat with two local young men, chatting over our 'minerals' – I had wondered why they had offered us a lump of metal – I began to realise they were a bit uneasy about something. Then I looked across the floor. Everyone was standing rigidly to attention, and quite a few were staring at our small group as if they couldn't believe their eyes. We got up. When in Rome, etc. Not that this allusion would have pleased everyone.

It was afterwards our conversation took a deeper turn. We learned that these Catholic young men had left school with good results but couldn't get a job that came anywhere near matching their qualifications. I was astounded. It was the late '50s, and I had no idea this was going on. So, I asked my partner, 'Why on earth do you put up with that? Can't you do something about it?'

His reply didn't really sink in. 'People are getting fed up. They often leave home to get a better job. But why should we have to? You're right. It's time we stopped letting ourselves be pushed around.'

That night someone pulled down all the red, white and blue bunting in Portstewart's main street that had been put up for the Orange Walk. My bloke? Perhaps. I have no idea, because I never saw him again. He had left me in a huff because my sympathy with his plight did not extend to letting him undo my bra. Mora and I had a good laugh at the idea he would find anything even if he had.

The next year Mora and I went to Bundoran and stayed in the Holyrood Hotel run by the McEniff family, already familiar to me from family visits. This was a laid-back establishment. Breakfasts started – and finished – later there than any other hotel I have ever visited, and the bar stayed open until the wee small hours. When one guest heading home missed the last train to Belfast, and returned fuming to the hotel, Mr McEniff calmed him down. 'Sure, there'll be another train tomorrow,' he pointed out. 'When the good God made time, He made plenty of it.'

In the evenings they had a showband, and we danced to country and western tunes. Jim Reeves' 'He'll Have to Go' was THE tune that summer. By day Mora and I got into our shorts and cycled around the country lanes. Showing our knees was considered pretty daring by the Irish holidaymakers. Then we went to the cinema one night to see *Some Like It Hot* with two young men from Dublin we had met at our hotel and shocked them with our unseemly hearty laughter at the scene aboard the yacht where Marilyn Monroe gets Tony Curtis's spectacles steamed up. A right pair of city slickers we were. On the last day of that holiday I received, to my astonishment, a proposal of marriage from Joe, the young Dublin man I had been seeing that fortnight. Only, he felt it was only fair to say, it would be a long engagement, as we would need to delay the wedding until he reached his 40th birthday at least, because only then could he afford to set up a home when he inherited a farm. I said no, wondering how to refuse him without hurting his feelings. I had just been enjoying his company and had no idea at all that he was feeling so serious. He had been very respectful, and my mum would have loved him. But I never was one of those city dwellers who dreams of rural living. And I just didn't want to marry him anyway.

Mora and I had travelled to Bundoran by rail and boat, but there was a seamen's strike at the end of the holiday, and the only way I could get back to work in time was to fly from Dublin. I phoned home, got my dad to wire me the necessary cash, and off I set by train to Dublin. I asked the taxi driver if he could recommend a respectable, cheap hotel for the night, and the one he suggested provoked hearty laughter in my young suitor, whom I had sought out to spend time with until my flight was due. It was the farmers' favourite hotel when they came for market day, and as such believed in Desperate Dan sized meals and very basic accommodation. Still unable to persuade me that marriage that far off was a good idea, Joe waved me off on my flight to Glasgow, saying 'Safe journey, God willing.'

This to someone who was only making her third ever journey on a plane. Nervous, me? Thanks to him I spent the entire hour's flight worrying about every whine and rumble made by the aircraft.

I decided that, apart from anything else, that much religiosity was not for me.

Everyone nowadays takes foreign holidays for granted, but in the early '60s it was an adventure. Spain had still to open up the Costas to any great extent, and many of us would not go there anyway while Franco remained in power. So another friend, Margie McGowan, who was in my Young Socialists branch and worked beside me in the gas board offices, set off with me for Rimini in Italy.

We took the Starlight Special overnight train to London, and then got on the express from Victoria to Dover to board the ferry across the Channel. Then for the first time in our lives we boarded a French train that took us through sunflower filled fields to Milan, where we changed to a local train with hard, wooden seats, heading for the resorts along the coast.

There were two priests from Birmingham in our hotel, who, to the bemusement of our waitress, tried to order their food in Latin, seeing Italian was derived from that language. Others just spoke in loud voices. One young couple with a ten month old baby asked the waitress if she would babysit to let them enjoy a night out. Margie and I were tickled to see the waitress out with her boyfriend, the said baby dandled on her knee, as they sat late at night in the café bar we had adopted as our favourite. This novel approach to babysitting was further demonstrated when the couple got up and danced to Chubby Checker's 'The Twist', baby held securely and gurgling with delight as they swayed from side to side and bobbed up and down.

Believing that missing Sunday Mass was a mortal sin, we asked where the church was, so we could go the next morning, and were met with astonished expressions. 'Why do you want to do that on your holiday? Only children and old women go to Mass.' That was the literal truth, as far as Rimini went anyway, as we observed in an almost empty church the following day.

Margie spoke fairly fluent Italian. All the better to fend off the ageing Lotharios – one of whom was a dead ringer for Rossano Brazzi – and the young Italian men in our own age group who seemed to think we must be available; otherwise why would we be on holiday without a chaperone? Margie's linguistic skills let her down one night, when she thought she had ordered her dancing partner, 'hands off'. He burst out laughing, saying, 'Why, have you got a gun?'

'Eh?'

'You said "hands up!"'

Our inexperience of another culture could have been our downfall. One night we accepted a lift back to our hotel from the two young men we had been dancing with in the café bar. At home this seemed a perfectly safe thing to do. I had often been seen home in Glasgow, and never felt myself in any danger whatsoever. But this night, instead of heading for our hotel, the driver tore off at great speed in the opposite direction into the countryside. Margie and I were terrified. I was envisioning murder and rape. We two young Catholic women brought up on the story of St Maria Goretti, who died from multiple stab wounds defending her honour at the age of 12, would certainly put up a fight. As the car sped along I tried to plan a strategy. Kick them where it hurt the most? Poke them in the eyes? We told them 'No, no,' loudly and firmly, over and over again, while the driver, one hand on the wheel, was trying to grope me with the other. Margie, in the back seat, was vehemently letting out a torrent of Italian as she fended off his pal.

I had no idea what she was saying, but it had an effect. The car stopped suddenly in the middle of an empty field, and they told us to get out. 'Here goes,' I thought. But instead of getting out too, they drove away, leaving Margie and me to hirple back to our hotel in our spiky-heeled dancing shoes. Moments earlier they might have had to serve us as weapons. As we walked along that country road, I asked Margie what she had been saying to them. 'Oh,' she replied airily, 'I told them your father was the assistant chief constable back home, and if anything happened to us...' We dissolved in laughter, but after that we were much more circumspect about our companions. Neat touch of authenticity, that. 'Chief constable' might not have been believed but adding 'assistant' gave it all the veracity it needed.

Others tried their luck, in a more gentle and civilised fashion, but got nowhere. The men we were going to marry were back home waiting for our return. But I'll give one hopeful the prize for being a romantic. We returned to our hotel late one night, and as we brushed our hair and washed off our make-up, I could hear a voice singing through the open window from down in the street below. 'Fiorella!' (little flower) he called. 'Please answer me.'

Sure enough, it was one of Margie's dancing partners serenading her. Much good did it do him.

Chapter 6

'St Trinian's, St Trinian's'

NOTRE DAME HIGH SCHOOL has lately been in the news, because it will no longer be the last remaining girls-only state school in Scotland. As a former pupil I support this change for the better.

My brothers always insisted that Notre Dame was Glasgow's version of St Trinian's. Here were hundreds of girls in box pleated gymslips, their school ties awry, who seemed to transform overnight into smart, well turned out young women in neat skirts and freshly ironed shirts. It was like caterpillars turning into butterflies. Yet there was one marked difference between Notre Dame and St Trinian's: we were not allowed to wear our skirts above mid-knee. The correct length was established by its skimming the floor when kneeling upright.

When I went for a year to the Montessori school, its primary feeder school named after Maria Montessori, the Italian educationalist, I looked forward to getting into the big school, which seemed to me like a day school copy of Enid Blyton's St Clare's, where boarding school pupils had page-turning adventures. Imagine, I would soon be playing hockey and netball. I'd have separate teachers for science, and languages, and everything. I could hardly wait. But first I would have to pass the Quali, the exam that decided our fates at the end of primary school.

This was long before comprehensives were created, and in Scotland education after the age of 11 was divided into senior secondaries for the children who had passed the Qualifying Examination, and junior secondaries for the large majority who had not. To divide children into sheep and goats at the age of 11 is manifestly absurd, but that's how it was.

Notre Dame High was selective – you had to do well in the dreaded 'Quali' to get in. My brother Jim, who had met former ND pupils at university, advised my parents to try to get me into the Montessori to improve my chances. Mum had left school at the age of 14. Her daughter was going to have the best education she could contrive.

I had to attend an interview with the Montessori's head teacher, so my mother planned I should be well-dressed for the occasion. She had made herself a New Look costume in green herring-boned tweed and draped around her shoulders was a tawny brown fox fur she had successfully bid for at an auction. She could not afford to get me a new coat, so she said her prayers and went to Paddy's Market, a flea market a step or two below The Barras. Lo and behold, she found not one, but two, nearly new coats, just my size. The one she chose for the interview was so ladylike, with its green loden wool, velvet collar and cloth covered buttons, you could imagine a princess wearing it on the balcony of Buckingham Palace. I was too much of a tomboy to feel altogether comfortable in it, but it suited my mother's purpose admirably. She even got me a straw bonnet with little pink rosebuds around the brim, and my new Clarks' sandals had not yet had time to get scuffed. This picture of demure girlhood was not far short of criminal misrepresentation, but it succeeded.

I am sure she must have won approval too. When the head teacher asked her why she wanted me to enter her school, my mother replied: 'I want my daughter to have the education I didn't have. And besides, when you educate a girl you educate a family.' Mum made me promise never to tell anyone that my coat came from Paddy's Market, but all these years later I hope she would forgive me, because I think her sheer guts and determination ought to be recognised.

She was ready, on my dad's tram driver's wage, to embark on the fantastic expense of buying schoolbooks, paying fees (modest as they were by other selective schools' standards) and splashing out on a uniform from Copland and Lye, outfitters to all the posh schools. That uniform included a black, long sleeved winter dress with a red collar. For summer it was a dress of cream tussore silk. Yes, silk! Then there was the blazer, a gabardine raincoat, a velour hat and a panama hat for summer. An optional extra was the purse with the school badge sewn on it, fastened to a long cord so that it could be hung around the neck.

That purse, or rather another girl's identical purse, brought me a day of utter misery not long after I started. I had forgotten to bring my sandshoes, so I had to stay behind in the classroom while everyone else went over to the convent where a large room was allocated for exercise with bean bags. I settled down comfortably to read the adventures of Penny and the Grey Ghosts in my *Girl's Crystal*.

On their return, Anna Vanni, one of my classmates, said her purse had gone missing from her desk. I had been alone in the room. Anna wasn't accusing me, but the fact remained the purse wasn't there and there had to be an explanation. Miss Gardner, the teacher, asked me if I had left my desk while they were all away, and I was worried in case they decided it must have been me and I got expelled before I had hardly started. And all that money wasted on the uniform, too. Such things happened in the school stories. I had never in my life committed any theft, but I sat there thinking they were bound to believe it was me, when all my classmates knew each other, and no-one had ever had anything stolen while at school before. I think, too, there was a glimmering of class consciousness in my pessimistic view. I was the new girl from a state primary, the others had been at this school from the age of five, and their daddies owned motor cars and were doctors and dentists and lawyers and businessmen. Miss Gardner said she would look into it further tomorrow, and meanwhile any girl who had taken it should take the chance to return it. For her part Anna was to look around carefully in case she had put it down somewhere else. I went home full of woe. But I returned the next day, determined to face whatever happened. Then Anna came in all smiles and told our teacher at once that she had never brought the purse to school at all. It had been at home all the time.

There was one particular girl in the class called Terry Curley who never doubted my word and had come over the day before to comfort and reassure me. She and I remained friends throughout our secondary years, enjoying a mutual love of trad jazz and jive. Terry had lively, laughing blue eyes, a mop of jet black hair, and was so petite she made everyone else feel large and clumsy. It was she who introduced me to Elinor Brent-Dyer's Chalet School books and Enid Blyton's stories of the twins at St Clare's, a less posh boarding school. Well, it's all relative, I suppose. Any boarding school seemed posh to me. Terry had been struck by polio when a young child, which left her with a limp, but she could out-jive anyone.

My next problem arose when Miss Gardner told me it was 'a bad, sad day when you came to this school'. Partly it was my behaviour. When a classmate stuck one of my pigtails in her inkwell I slapped her on the face. And my arithmetic was not as good as she had been led to believe. At St Conval's, my local primary school, I had been considered a star, and I was determined to show her. The incident with the purse strengthened my resolve. So I asked Joe to give me practice in mental arithmetic and the times tables. I got an S1, the top band in the Quali, and won the arithmetic prize. The day it was awarded Miss Gardner seemed as delighted as me. If she had been using a ploy to get me to put in more effort, she had certainly succeeded. I was even behaving in a more ladylike fashion.

My mother attributed my success to her prayers to the Blessed Virgin Mary, but scepticism had been growing in my mind. I was troubled by the story of Abraham and Isaac and would not let go of it until Mum and Dad promised they would never kill me to please God, but in any case He wouldn't ask them to do any such thing. So why, I persisted, did He ask Abraham? They replied that, as God knew everything, He would know that Abraham would do as he was bid, but He, God, would not actually want him to do it. I told myself maybe it was just a story.

Then, when Miss Gardner said tartly one day to a girl who was praying for success in the Quali that 'God helps those who help themselves', I decided to be a religious rebel on the quiet. I would not say any prayers, but would work hard, and see what happened.

So then I was off to Notre Dame High School, founded in 1897, and run by the Sisters of Notre Dame, a teaching order founded in France that had schools around the world at large. The school badge bore the motto, 'Ah, qu'Il est bon, le Bon Dieu', a favourite saying of the founder, and translated by generations of disrespectful schoolgirls as 'What good is the good God?'

As well as the aforementioned gym slips tied around the waist with a blue, yellow, green or red sash according to our house colour there was the blue shirt, a blue and yellow striped tie that was knotted at the start of the term and thereafter slid up and down instead of being re-knotted every day, a blue dress for the summer months, a brown blazer with the school badge and yellow and blue trimming down the lapels, a velour winter hat and a panama hat for summer. For gym we wore a brown cotton tunic – all we needed was Jesus sandals to play the slaves in any film set in Ancient Rome.

Some of the girls wore berets instead of hats, a concession left over from the days of wartime scarcities, but the nuns didn't like them and did their utmost to reassert the old standards. Not a war they won. The berets stayed.

It was not long before I was questioning the common sense of a few of my mentors. In the summer months of that first year we did not wear the blue uniform dress that was later to be imposed, but any blue dress of our choice. My mother applied herself once again to her sewing machine and produced two beautiful dresses. Then calamity struck. Sister Julie, my form teacher, told me that one of them was immodest and I was not to wear it to school anymore. Immodest? I didn't understand. What was wrong with it? She pointed to its little voile insert, about four inches by three, just under my neck. 'I can see your skin through that,' she said. My mother was mortified, but also sorely puzzled. Modesty was the greatest virtue in her eyes. I had nothing to be modest about. I was 11 years old and as boyish of figure as it was possible to be. Then a few months later Sister Mary Anthony, the head teacher, decreed we had to wear a uniform dress that was devoid of any attractive feature, ridiculously expensive, and creased when you had it on for five minutes. I was all the more annoyed because I knew how difficult my parents found it to pay for all the costs of my education.

Another one of the nuns told me not to whistle tunes as I walked down the corridor, an irritating accomplishment I had been taught by my brothers. Not because it got on her wick, which I would have accepted as reasonable; it was because Our Lady cried when girls whistled. Eh?

'And what is that tune you've been whistling, anyway?' she asked.

'"The St Louis Blues March", Sister', I replied.

'Well, stop it, and don't do it again.'

'OK Sister. Oh, sorry, Sister. I didn't mean sister like that, Sister, I meant "sister" the way you're a sister...' I trailed off.

'What on earth are you talking about, Maria?' she asked.

'I mean, in America, someone talking to a lady might call her "sister".'

'I am aware that in America a female who is not a nun might be addressed as "sister", but what has that got to do with here and now?'

'Because it's an American tune I was whistling, Sister. That's what made me think of it.'

'I really don't know what goes through that mind of yours, Maria,' she said, shaking her head as she walked away.

One day Sister Ignatius, in vindication of her belief that modern youth was lazier than previous generations, asked the class how many of us washed and ironed our uniforms. I put my hand up and then realised no-one else was doing so. The reason was every other family had a washing machine, and there was no point in not throwing in the uniform with the rest of the wash. Around that time, too, my mother was anticipating a hysterectomy operation. With all the advances made since then, this is still major surgery. My mother was in no fit state to do ordinary household tasks, so I not only did my laundry but quite a lot of the household chores as well. Before she went into hospital she was suffering from very heavy bleeding and was virtually housebound, so I had to buy sanitary towels for her. Such was my introduction to the onset of puberty, which I hated because it was another constraint on my liberty, and the period pains were bloody sore to boot. When she recovered consciousness in her hospital bed, and was informed the operation had gone well, she assured the surgeon it was all down to the Blessed Virgin Mary. I suppose he must have been used to patients who had such airy disregard for his skills.

I cannot remember a time when my mother was not on medication for something-or-other. In early childhood I was warned not to open her box of Phenobarbitone pills, a sedative for her nerves, but not one they prescribe nowadays. Although she had high blood pressure since she was in her early 40s, she certainly never cut back on salt. She was always a bit overweight. There was far less effective medication for high blood pressure then, so you would think it would have been all the more important to emphasise a healthy lifestyle to try to bring it down. But maybe they did, and she didn't pay any attention. 'Doctors – what do they know?' she would say.

Around this time, I first experienced political confrontation. I didn't have any notion that this was to be my life's path. It was 1951, and Sister Julie, whose normal practice was to ask us to pray for someone's intentions, asked the class that day to pray for a Conservative victory in the coming General Election. My lips stayed firmly shut, and she noticed but she did not say anything. Why was I, at the age of 12, adamant I would not pray for any such thing? Obvious, really. All my family were Labour. They had benefited from Clement Attlee's government in ways they would never have seen under the Tories. The creation of the NHS. Their new home. In the newspapers I saw large, expensive adverts picturing 'Mr Cube', a cartoon character invented by the British sugar industry, aimed at preventing its nationalisation by the Labour Government. Far from warming to Mr Cube I just felt annoyed that these people used such vast amounts of money to attack the Labour Government.

She must have thought God had delivered. The Conservatives won 302 seats with a total of 12,660,061 votes. Labour had considerably more votes – 13,948,883 – its biggest vote in its entire history to date – but won only 295 seats. And it's seats that count, not the tally of votes. Labour lost this election with around two million more votes than they won in the 1945 landslide. Down through the years lazy (or deliberately deceitful?) political writers have asserted that Labour lost the people's confidence in 1951 on account of the continuing rationing and shortages, but these figures show that is simply not true.

Experienced teachers can recognise their pupils' time-wasting ruses. Sister Julie had not then, it would seem, acquired that skill. One day a bored classmate, reluctant to know any more about the rivers of Europe, asked her to tell us how she became a nun. Tapping her pointer on Africa's Mediterranean coast on the wall map as she spoke, Sister Julie told us she had had a boyfriend who fought at El Alamein. While he was away his letters dried up, and she wondered if he was cooling off. I sat thinking death would have been a likely explanation. Meanwhile her chum, hoping to be accepted as a postulant at the local Notre Dame convent, had been invited to an interview with the Mother Superior, and she agreed to accompany her nervous friend. The visit to the convent attracted her to the life of a nun. But she was fond of her boyfriend. What to do? She decided to apply to the convent, and whichever letter she got first, the convent's or the boyfriend's, she would take as a sign from God of what He wanted her to do. Not entirely surprisingly, the convent's letter, posted in the same city, arrived soon after. The next day the postman brought a bundle of letters from North Africa. They had probably been held up by the army censors, checking for information that could help the enemy. Or maybe just the difficulties of getting mail out of a war zone. But God had spoken. I sat there dumbfounded, saying to myself, 'This eejit is in charge of me, and I have more common sense than she has.' Many years later I recalled this story one night over our evening meal in the House of Commons, where a group of Scottish Labour MPs would frequently get together, and we were regaling each other with tales of the allegedly best days of our life. John Home Robertson argued that God had indeed intervened. He had saved this poor soldier from coming home to marry such a silly woman.

For years, kneeling on the lino, I had spoken to God and his legions of saints, but now my first Doubts with a capital 'D' began. There was a film that came out in the early '50s that told the story of the miracle of Fátima. Fátima is a village in Portugal where, around the time of the First World War and the Russian Revolution, some local children claimed they had seen visions of the Virgin Mary, and she had told them she would give the world a sign. A large crowd assembled on a hillside to witness what that might be. According to reports of the event, they saw the sun come down in the sky, nearer and nearer to earth, and everyone was terrified until they saw it reverse and go back up again.

Doubting Thomasina, as I was dubbed by Sister Ignatius, was having none of it. 'How could that happen,' I asked, 'without other people around the part of the world that was in daylight noticing?'

'That is the miracle.'

'Why not do it so that everybody notices, and then they'd all believe?'

'If we had proof, there would be no need for faith.'

'But if the sun really moved towards the earth, wouldn't the planets be thrown out of their orbits?'

'God, being God, is all-powerful. He can make the apparently impossible happen. He created the solar system, so He can make the sun move and not move at the same time.'

I wouldn't budge. The Monsignor who visited the school to give us additional religious instruction was asked to have a quiet word with me. He went through the arguments, but in the end told me belief in Fátima was not an article of faith. In other words, I could be a Catholic and not believe it. But many pious people did, and it was better not to upset them.

There were aspects of my school life I did enjoy. In the weeks before Christmas we stayed behind after school, in a small room in the convent, to make flowers out of crepe paper for sale at the bazaar to indulgent parents. We played charades – a new game to me. We learned unfamiliar carols, like the mediaeval 'I Sing of a Maiden'. I can never hear 'The Holly and the Ivy' without thinking of winter days in that classroom, looking out at the snow on the rooftops.

Each year had its choir, and Miss McCabe, the choir mistress, known to us as 'Maccabee', expected high standards, but was a true democrat. One year she brought in the sheet music for 'I Know My Love', a traditional Irish melody, but as soon as we read the words we protested. What kind of doormat was this, singing:

There is a dance house in Maradyke
Where my true love goes every night
And takes a strange girl upon his knee
And don't you know, now, that vexes me.
And still she cried, 'I love him the best'
But a troubled mind, sure, can get no rest.
And still she cried, 'Bonny boys are few,
But if my love leaves me what will I do?'

This had nothing in common with modern girls like us. If that was our boyfriend, we would tell him to take a running jump. Maccabee gave in and took the sheet music back to the shop. But she was no softie, and not one to listen to feeble excuses. Two of my classmates, late for practice one day, attempted to get out of trouble by claiming they had been praying in the chapel and had not noticed the time going by. She observed, sarcasm dripping from every word, 'You'll grow up into the kind of women who will be praying when you should be making your husband's dinner!'

Although I had my disagreements with Sister Julie, I will give her this credit: she put on highly popular free film shows. Stewart Granger's Rider Haggard adventures were great favourites. We would settle into our chairs with the choc ices she had supplied and revel in these fantasies. Groans would go up whenever the film stopped. Sister Julie protested she was only changing reels, but we suspected she was censoring the kissing bits.

Nowadays children go on school trips to places we would have thought too exotic to contemplate. Our first school trip was to Iona, and on that lovely, tranquil island there were no shops and nothing to spend our pocket money on. But eggs were still rationed, and I discovered that the islanders had notices at their farm gates saying they had eggs for sale without coupons. The perfect present for Mum and Dad! Soon the whole island was cleaned out, but this minor exercise in entrepreneurship met disapproval from our teachers. We were on Iona to pray and think about Christianity being brought to our land, not go combing the island to buy eggs.

I had a similar experience of minds not quite meeting when we had a retreat. Told that we could bring reading matter, provided it was something spiritual like the life of a saint, and not any other kind of books, I brought a pack of my brother Joe's playing cards instead, and was happily teaching my friends how to play poker when it was explained to me that this was not considered appropriate.

My imagination was fired by our school's old red sandstone building, and I didn't care for the new, yellow brick building that was opened in 1953. The old building had nooks and crannies to explore, and a long gloomy corridor to the convent chapel inhabited by a friendly smoky grey Persian cat, which was fond of walking around the altar, getting under the priest's feet during Benediction. Sometimes we noticed a collection of shoes lying at the bottom of the staircase that led to the nuns' cells, and rumour had it that the nuns, as an act of penance, wore other people's shoes no matter whether they were too large or too tight. There was one wee nun who loved to fill the altar and the steps leading up to it with umpteen vases of flowers. I can see her now, fussing over her roses, dahlias and lilies. She was visibly upset when the priest got irritated with having to negotiate his way around these obstacles and declared heatedly on the altar steps that he would have more room to move in a flower shop.

I have sometimes been asked if I considered a political career when at school. The thought never entered my head, although I had experience of winning votes as vice-captain of St Columba's House. The teachers appointed the captains of the Houses. There were no duties attached to the vice-captaincy, other than being a shop steward, insofar as you dared, for your classmates. Points could be won or lost, and the athletic amongst us won points galore. I could jump high from a standing start, so I was put in defence at netball, but I was never to be in the school team because I would stand daydreaming until agitated screams from teammates drew my attention to the ball's approach. 'Binkie' MacLean, our PE teacher, would ask me in exasperation what I found so interesting as I gazed beyond the netball pitch. My daydreams were of being a reporter and phoning the editor to hold the front page while I delivered my scoop. In my spare time I would write the next Glasgow novel. Meanwhile I regularly wrote for the school magazine.

1956 was my last year in school, during which my interest in politics began. That was the year of Suez, Cyprus and the Hungarian Uprising. Suez was debated hotly throughout the land. Nasser had been elected President of Egypt and sought closer links with Russia. The West withdrew its help with the Aswan Dam, whereupon Nasser took over the Suez canal. The Israelis and the French, supported by the United Kingdom, moved against Nasser. There was such a row in the Labour Party about it that fisticuffs broke out on the floor of the party conference. Aneurin Bevan spoke out against our bombing Egypt to a huge crowd in Trafalgar Square:

> Sir Anthony Eden has been pretending that he is now invading Egypt in order to strengthen the United Nations. Every burglar of course could say the same thing, he could argue that he was entering the house in order to train the police. So, if Sir Anthony Eden is sincere in what he is saying, and he may be, he may be, then if he is sincere in what he is saying then he is too stupid to be a Prime Minister.

That was the stuff to give them.

In the end the USA stepped in to bring an end to this venture. Not that we were entirely happy with the USA. That was the year when the first H-bomb was tested at Bikini Atoll.

Rock 'n' Roll had a response. Bill Haley & His Comets sang 'Thirteen Women'. The theme of the song was the aftermath of an H-bomb war, in which there were 13 women and only one man in town. Does this hold the record for the silliest pop song ever written? What seems an amazing misjudgement on Decca's part is that 'Rock around the Clock' was the B-side of this disc. Moon-faced, tubby, kiss-curled Bill Haley was a rock 'n' roll idol.

My own idol was Lonnie Donegan, a Glasgow man who at that time played banjo and guitar with Chris Barber's jazz band and had still to find international fame. I bought *New Musical Express* every week just so that I could cut out his pictures. The night I heard 'Rock Island Line' for the first time on the radio I was filled with excitement and rushed into school the next day to talk about it. What was so great about it? It was different. We were fed up with crooners who had nothing new to say. We were living in a pop revolution and did not realise it.

Chapter 7

'Let's Go to the Hop'

THEY SAY NO one ever forgets their first love. I will not forget my first date. I was 17 and I had been asked to go to the pictures by a young man called Harry I had met at a St Mungo's school dance.

I don't know whether Harry was on his first date too. If he was ill at ease he didn't show it. I certainly was, and it didn't help that my brother Joe was singing 'I'm Just Wild About Harry' as I stood at the living room window waiting for my bus to appear, having changed into three different dresses. This was typical of Joe. When I came downstairs wearing a yellow shirt dress for my first school dance he declaimed, 'Say howdy to the queen of the southern belles. It's the cutie from Custard Creek.' That dance was memorable for one of my classmates being sent home by a nun supervising us for wearing an immodest dress. The hussy was wearing a frock with little cap sleeves showing nearly all her arms. Whatever next?

Harry's choice of film was, oh no, *And God Created Woman*, starring the new sex kitten sensation Brigitte Bardot. He took my right hand in his and held it. And kept on holding it. I was beginning to wonder if I could blow my nose with my left hand. I was also beginning to realise that holding hands is something you do if you feel the urge, and it's no enjoyment at all if you don't. He put his arm around my shoulder. I sat as stiff as a board, worrying in case some embarrassing scene would crop up. But worse than that, the day before I had been hit in the mouth by a cricket ball. I had been talked into joining some local kids to make up the numbers for their game of rounders, and when the ball hit me I felt a tooth slacken. Then it fell out. I kept fretting in case my date noticed the gap and decided I looked like a witch, so every time I smiled I kept my lips closed. But I wasn't all that attracted to him really. Pleasant company and quite good looking, but we seemed to have little or nothing in common. He fell short of the standard set by Lonnie Donegan. I was no Brigitte Bardot either.

My mother thought Catholic boys would be more 'respectful' than Protestants. Other, non-Christian religions were so far beyond the pale they were not even contemplated. Not respectful was a thought so dire she could not bring herself to be explicit. She need not have worried. I was less frightened of becoming an unmarried mother – in those days a terrible disgrace often covered up by the grandmother pretending to be the baby's mother – than of going to Hell for all eternity. Not that my mother would have pretended any such thing. Hard to see how she could, when all the neighbours knew she had had a hysterectomy.

Eternal damnation, burning in the fires of Hell, was the real worry. If you died in a state of mortal sin, not having been to confession and repented, then that was what God had in store for you. No one, after all, knew the day or the hour they could fall under a bus, or be felled by some fatal illness before they had time to make their confession and carry out their penance. The Devil was constantly on the lookout, tempting people into sin. Besides, the priests at St Conval's knew my voice and I'd be too embarrassed to tell them anything like that. Of course, I could go to another chapel where I was not known, but that seemed like cheating.

At school we had set out to discomfit our mentors by asking 'How far can you go?' – without committing mortal sin, that is. Not far at all, it would seem. Besides looking after our own souls, we girls were apparently responsible for safeguarding the opposite sex's souls, and therefore had to avoid occasions of sin. The male sex were apparently less able to control their urges than the female, so there was a lot for us to be careful about. How we dressed, how we spoke, what we drank, where we went – there seemed no end to it.

I was so terrified of becoming pregnant that every month I anxiously awaited my period, even although I knew I could not possibly be pregnant. Logic and common sense told me, again and again, it was impossible. My anxiety was not a matter of worrying in case precautions (that would have been sinful in themselves) did not work. It was impossible simply because I had yet to take that necessary step without which one cannot conceive. There had been only one virgin birth I had ever heard of, and no one with large wings called Gabriel had been to visit me. My superstitious dread could still not be ignored.

Mum's idea of a suitable boyfriend had me running for cover. He came to the door every Sunday afternoon to collect our contribution to the church building fund. Not that he asked me out anyway. But Mum thought it was only a matter of time until he got up his courage. How could he possibly not be attracted to her daughter? He probably only did the collection, she thought, so he could see me. I hadn't at first realised why I was always left to be the one to answer his knock. Mum would say to me, 'That's a fine young man, but he's quite shy. I'm sure he wants to ask you out, but you – you can't shut the door on him fast enough. He's nice and steady, with a good job. He'd be a good husband.' And I would reply in irritation, 'But I don't want to go out with him. He's too holy.' That was probably unfair, and he must have had a heart of gold. This good and kindly soul used up his holiday leave every year taking sick people to Lourdes. Highly admirable, I do realise, but I was certain this was not the life for me.

It's sometimes the trivial things that matter. In the early sixties' I got serious with one boyfriend in particular, who was great company, but he always had three pristine white handkerchiefs in his pockets that his mother had ironed for him. One for when he needed to blow his nose, the second for anyone else who might need to, and the third for show, neatly folded in his breast pocket. I, on the other hand, regarded the paper tissue as one of the great inventions of the 20th century. His mother, a woman of depressingly high standards when it came to housekeeping, ironed everything for him. I stood in their kitchen one day watching her iron his underpants. I thought there was no way I could live up to this.

Then one night he told me he wanted to marry me, but there was an important snag. He felt he could not marry a Catholic. He couldn't bear to get married in a Catholic church. His view of Catholicism was coloured by the role of the Church in supporting Franco in the Spanish Civil War, and the undue influence of the priests in Ireland. But here we were, living not in the Spain of our parents' generation, or in some rural village in Ireland where the priest ruled the roost, but in modern Scotland. I did try to talk him round, but it was useless.

Although I had a lot of doctrinal doubts his view seemed unbalanced and unfair to me. Indifference I could have lived with. And wait a minute, I said to myself, if he detests the religion that has been part of the making of the person I am, what else will it be next? I might be heading more and more away from the beliefs in which I was raised, but I'll decide when and if I ever leave it on grounds of changed beliefs, not to please someone else. And anyway, I hate ironing.

I talked it over with my mum and dad, because in spite of my joking to myself about the ironing I really was very unhappy. They had been displeased over my going out with a non-Catholic, but they understood my sorrow. Dad felt I was showing my head was screwed on right and praised me for my clear thinking. 'Marriage is demanding enough,' he said, 'when you have everything in common.' Mum said, 'He just wasn't the right one for you anyway. Someone else will come along, you'll see.' And my pals said, 'Takes a man to cure a man. Come on out to the dancing.'

Earlier on, when schooldays were over I began studies at the Scottish College of Commerce, and Peter, a law student, entered my life at its Christmas dance. He sought to flatter me when he said there was no point in my staying in to study for my exams, as someone with my looks could easily marry somebody rich. This attitude annoyed me. For one thing, men on their way to their first million weren't exactly beating a path to my door in Pollok. And I was no gold digger anyway.

I would have given him up there and then, but Mum was upset because I was going out with a Protestant. If I stopped seeing him she'd think she had won. Then Peter's face was in the evening paper because he had been awarded a medal for best student of his year, and Mum realised what a good catch he was. Peter was only attached to the Church of Scotland by a flimsy thread, and this gave her hope. 'Do you think he would turn?' she asked me. He had not, it has to be said, ever mentioned any marital intentions, but Mum was sure he would.

Even if I had wanted to marry him, I would not raise the subject. I hated the idea of people insincerely converting to any religion just so they could get married. Part of the pressure to seek the conversion of one's intended was that a nuptial mass was only possible if the couple were both Catholics. If one or the other was not, there would only be a shortened ceremony, with no music, in the vestry and not before the altar. What was supposed to be a joyful occasion was treated as if it was something to deplore. But I stopped seeing Peter because while he was working hard enough on his own career to ensure outstanding success he couldn't take my own need to pass seriously. Most of all I realised it was silly, and unfair to any man, to keep going out with him just to defy my mother.

Another young man passed muster with my mother because he came from a good Catholic family of her acquaintance. When we went out together we would usually see a film. No hand holding, no arm around the shoulder. Then he would see me home to my garden gate, tell me what a nice time he had had, say goodnight, and leave without so much as a peck on the cheek. This went on for several weeks, so I asked my brother Joe if he thought this was a bit unusual. I did not ask Mum. She would have thought this was exactly the kind of respectful behaviour that she approved. Joe agreed it certainly was a bit odd, but maybe he was just a bit backward at coming forward. A week or two would resolve it one way or the other.

Then one night this young man and I were discussing our hopes and dreams for the future, and he told me he intended to be a priest. I couldn't have been more surprised if he'd said he was a Martian. 'In that case', said I, when I had recovered my wits, 'don't you think we shouldn't be going out together?' The very idea of dating a would-be priest and presenting any kind of obstacle to his vocation – it was out of the question. His answer stunned me. 'Oh, but you see, I want to test my vocation.'

'Not with me, you won't', I said to myself, and it was off to the dancing to find someone else. He really did become a priest, and the last I heard of him he was somewhere in Latin America, supporting peasants fighting for their rights.

This experience gave me an idea. I always found it difficult to tell a young man I no longer wanted to see him. The younger generation today have a better attitude: if a couple doesn't hit it off it's no big deal. My generation would agonise over it. It seemed to imply a criticism, when all that may have been wrong was an incompatibility of personalities. So I would tell him I was considering becoming a nun. The most blatant lie I have ever told, and not one that would have been believed by anyone who really knew me. Still, it worked.

My brother Jim was given the elbow for a reason that I had never heard before or since. His girlfriend told him one night that she was fond of him, and really liked him a lot, but she wanted a more peaceful life. He was always raising topics of conversation she had never thought about and didn't want to bother thinking about. Going out with him was too much like hard work. Jim had met fierce, unrelenting opposition from our parents every time he went out with a non-Catholic girl. My mother would take to her bed, declaring herself ill from the worry of it all. He ended up emigrating to America: partly to make a good career move in the newly-developing computer world, but partly also to get away from parental control. But isn't this all too typical. Joanne, his first wife, was more like our mother than anyone else I have ever met. She even directed him on what shoes to wear with his suit, which Jim didn't seem to mind, but I would have found intolerable. The man I married, Jim Fyfe, had a dress sense that could have been kindly described as shambolic, but neither he nor I cared. He would ruin every jacket he ever had in no time, stuffing the pockets with books and newspapers. I found this endearing. Joanne would have been giving him daily lectures.

When it came his turn for parental review of his girlfriends, Joe (who had been observing his elder brother's travails) just said to them, 'This is not for discussion', and did what he liked. At that time, I was going to a ballroom dancing class that Joe already attended where he had started dating a girl called Margaret, and so I later acquired a great sister-in-law.

In due course I had the same rows, and although in the end I got married to Jim, who was a Catholic, from a good Catholic family, he still met censure. He was not a good enough Catholic in my mother's eyes. He did not suggest going to Benediction when we were out on Sunday nights, as my parents had done during their courtship. I thought it better not to point out that if either Jim or I had found the other to be the kind of person whose idea of a good Sunday evening was a visit to the church, each of us would have fled.

When Jim made his first visit to my family home it was a wonder he ever came back. Mum spent the evening regaling him with the career successes of my past boyfriends, and during the dinner, as his knife went into the red meat, she gave him a graphic description of the operation she recently had. Being used to it, I didn't get queasy at this kind of conversation, but Jim's lively imagination saw everything in Technicolor and 3D, and he had to force his food down.

But Jim was not to be put off. He would see me home, we would have a kiss and cuddle at my garden gate, and then he would run up the hill to get the last bus back to the city centre, from where he would walk miles all the way to where he lived in Balornock. When Jim came along I just knew he was the one. But more of that later.

My teens and early 20s were a time when ballroom dancing – the quickstep, foxtrot, tango and modern waltz – were essential skills. There might be an occasional samba or rumba, or the new mambo, and in some of the more relaxed dancehalls there would be a corner set aside for jiving. But everyone had to know the basic steps, and it was a pest to have a partner who did not and kept treading on your toes. You had to dress up to go out dancing, even to the simplest hop at a local hall. The fashion was to have a wide skirt, under which it was essential to have no fewer than three stiff net petticoats to achieve maximum sticky-outiness. The net was so rough it snagged your brand new nylons, but who cared? If I didn't smoke I could have money to burn on stockings, make-up, perfume and 78 RPM records. Not without an envious pang, however. My pal Mora acquired instant chic smoking her Gauloises cigarettes, each one having a different coloured paper.

This was the era of the Teddy Boys, 'Edwardian' suits in bright colours, and DA haircuts. I didn't like this style. Men's fashions were not something I paid much attention to, but I noticed something odd going on amongst the guys I knew in Govan and Gorbals Young Socialists (YS) through my membership of Craigton YS, the youth wing of the Labour Party which I had joined in the aftermath of the 1959 defeat. Gus Macdonald, Joe O'Brien, and their pals, young apprentices who were highly clothes conscious, didn't like these pink and sky blue suits with velvet collars either. So they decided to spend their wages on something entirely different. They went to a local tailor's shop owned by Harry Selby, who was their political guru and had a brief career as an MP. What must he have thought of their request? They wanted to dress like Mississippi gamblers, with three buttoned draped jackets in dark colours. That length of Harris Tweed languishing unsold on the shelf would do nicely. Pat Lally (of whom more later) did the tailoring and Perry Como haircuts completed the look. They called it the 'moonie', and it was a forerunner to the mods that came along years later. There was no female equivalent of this. My pals and I all became weekend beatniks, and I went around in black polo necked jumpers, my long straight black hair hanging down my back.

We made a point of frequenting just about every ballroom around, and there were plenty of them. The Plaza at Eglinton Toll at the upper end of the market had a fountain in the middle of the dance floor, and everyone waltzed or quickstepped their way around it. Warren's Albert Ballroom in Bath Street was where serious dancers congregated to practise for the competitions that were held there. Green's Playhouse (which later became the Apollo) at the top of Renfield Street had a visiting band called Dr Crock and the Crackpots, and Joe Loss played there for years and years. Barrowland was downmarket from these others but highly popular, and away from the city centre there was the Dennistoun Palais in the east end, and the Flamingo out along Paisley Road West, which had a rock 'n' roll corner when other ballrooms were keeping this new phenomenon at bay.

But the Locarno was the one with worldwide fame. Visiting soldiers, sailors and airmen always knew where to go and made a bee-line for the Locarno. One such, with happy memories of his days in Scotland, later became a colleague of my brother Jim in Los Angeles, where he had gone to work as an engineer designing fuselages for McDonnell Douglas. He asked him in all seriousness how he had ever brought himself to leave a place that contained such delights as the Locarno.

When I worked in the Scottish Gas Board office in George Square, the junior in my department dated an American sailor she had met at the Locarno, called Jack. Then when naval duties took him away temporarily, she met another American sailor when out dancing at the same spot, also called Jack. At a later stage she decided she wanted to keep seeing one of them, but not the other. When an American drawl on the office phone asked for her we were in a quandary wondering if this was the one she wanted to put through or the one she wanted to dump.

The student unions had regular dances. Our own college had an occasional dance, only enlivened by the presence of some Arab students who thought they had died and gone to heaven, with all these western girls around. One of them used to sit, curled up in an ancient armchair, in a corner of the common room. When I entered the room one morning, and saw him looking woebegone, I asked him how he was. He shook his head mournfully and replied, 'Soffering.' His big brown eyes looked at me soulfully.

What do you mean, Mehemet, you're suffering? What's up with you?'

'I am soffering, because you will not go out with me.'

'Not likely. I don't want to be another one of your conquests.'

'Maria, Maria, I beg you. It would not be like that. I would loff you and you alone for ever more.'

Then my pal Betty walked in. 'How's things, Mehemet?'

'Soffering.'

That January we took part in student charities day. It had been snowing for days, and the Indian students had never seen this phenomenon. They couldn't stop lifting handfuls of the stuff and loved a snowball fight. They skipped a lecture to build a snowman out in the street. Charities Day used to be a regular event in the Glasgow calendar, when 'thae daft students' from the university and all the colleges would get into fancy dress and rattle tin collecting cans in the street, on buses, and in the shops. The male students would chase attractive girls, having them screaming with laughter, determined to get them to put some coins in their can.

The cans, well filled by a generous Glasgow public, always bore a punning slogan like 'Philip McCann'. More cash still rolled in from the sale of a magazine put together by the students, full of tasteless jokes, that would be ensured good sales when someone in authority condemned it. Our team got into Roman togas, and on the concourse of Central Station performed a jive formation to the tune of 'Rock Around the Clock'. We gathered a good collection every time the music stopped.

The art school dance was as bohemian as you would expect. One night when the clip holding up my long hair broke I had to let it fall as it would. That may have had nothing to do with it, but I had my best night ever. I didn't sit out a single dance.

And then there was Glasgow University Men's Union. In its defence it has to be said it was the only one that occasionally hired Chris Barber's Trad Jazz Band, and I would put up with a lot for that. I had the obsessive knowledge of the band's line-up and their previous histories that is usually observed in footie fanatics. I still remember: Pat Halcox on trumpet, Monty Sunshine on clarinet, Barber on trombone, Dick Smith on bass, Ron Bowden on drums, Lonnie Donegan on banjo and guitar, and the glamorous Ottilie Patterson singing, the fringes on her black tunic dress swinging as she gave it laldy.

Other trad jazz bands visited too. My brother Jim worried in case I ran away with a bass player I was always enthusing about. This amazed me because I didn't think anyone – least of all my own brother – would believe I was that stupid. When he – the musician, that is – turned up at my school at four o'clock one day in a red sports car I got my pals to pretend I wasn't there. At ten years older than me, he was probably married.

The downside of the men's union was their resident band. It

was abominable. They would play non-stop for maybe 20 minutes, then rest for ten. If you were dancing with someone you were not attracted to, but had been too polite to refuse, that was a whole half-hour wasted. Their music was the standards of the '30s and '40s: they never made the slightest attempt to get up to date. I'm telling you, it was weird having some spotty youth who fancied himself as a smoothie crooning 'Moonlight Becomes You' into your ear as we circled around the floor. Then there were the awful chat-up lines.

'Where have you been all my life?'

'Hiding,' I would reply.

'Do you come here often? You do? So how come I've missed the most beautiful girl here?' Oh please.

Then there was the one that every Glaswegian has heard.

'Has anyone ever told you you're one in a million?'

'So's your chances.'

There were two basic expected responses. Either the girl would dissolve in giggles, saying, 'Oh, you are awful' – as Dick Emery satirised it. Or she would give a snappy reply back, which made her partner laugh. My husband Jim and I found we made each other laugh. But some of the student Lotharios just wanted to consider themselves a hell of a fellow.

A favourite opening gambit at these uni dances was, 'Do you believe in free love?' That this was an extremely odd way to begin a conversation with someone you have just met for the first time never seemed to occur to them. One of my pals, Rosemary Thomson, found it hilarious seeing their faces when she replied, 'No, but my charges are reasonable', but her older sister made her stop it.

Another young man wanted to know whether, when I took a bath, did I face the taps or have my back to them? 'Why do you want to know?' I asked, walking right into it.

'So that I can picture you accurately.'

A few thought it a good idea to walk up to a girl, look her slowly up and down from head to foot, and then having satisfied his scrutiny ask her to dance. My pal Margaret Hagan had the perfect response to this. She would look him up and down equally slowly, shaking her head slightly at different parts of his anatomy, and then say 'No thanks'.

I had thought until recently that awful chat-up lines were a thing of the past, but no. Only a few years ago I learned that a young man might declare his attraction with the sweet and tender words: 'Get your coat on, you've pulled'. And here's another, which was actually voted in some poll or other as the most effective: 'This time next year we'll be laughing together.' Implies commitment, you see. But if the girl is a bit more streetwise than her suitor believes, she might respond, in time-honoured fashion as her mother and grandmother did before her: 'Yir patter's like watter.'

Only recently I have heard of one that was new to me: 'Did it hurt when you fell out of Heaven?' I wonder what I would have said. Maybe, 'Don't remember. No baby can.'

Meantime, what was happening to my school pals? Betty got married, and later divorced. She was the first girl from my school to do that. Up until then everyone I knew thought that when you married it was a case of 'you've made your bed, now lie in it.' No matter how bad a mistake it was.

Mora landed lucky, although it did not seem so at first. One day she phoned to tell me she wanted to kick herself from here to Timbuktu. She had been out with a new boyfriend on a first date and had tripped on the cinema steps and put a hole in her stocking. She felt clumsy and embarrassed and was sure he would not phone her again. But I knew Mora better than that. She had the gift of calmness in all manner of situations. I was sure that she would have carried off any such small difficulty with aplomb. Later on, I met Brian, who told me how he had been impressed by her composure, and by her outstanding achievement in graduating when she was only 19. They were a perfect match for each other and lived a long and happy life together until Mora's fatal illness some years ago.

But before Brian had come along Mora's dad took a hard-line on boyfriends crossing the threshold of his house. He told her firmly, 'I don't want an endless procession of callow youths coming into my house. When you begin seeing men you might consider marrying then that will be the time to start.'

Above: Maria's mother as a young woman, manager of a licensed grocer.

Right: Cox and Cusick, the stars of Maria's parents' concert party, The Sunbeams.

Left: Maria, aged ten, with her parents in Dunoon. The straw bonnet is part of the story.

Below: Maria's parents' wedding photo. There is a reason for the tear omitting the best man.

Left: Maria's First Holy Communion, in a dress and cloak made my her mother.

Above: Maria celebrating her success in the 'Quali'.

Left: Maria wearing her 'terrible' Notre Dame uniform, 1954.

Maria and her brother, Joe, on holiday on the Isle of Man.

The young women who won equal pay at the Scottish Gas Board. The Scottish Gas Board no longer exists. Maria is fourth from the left.

Above: Maria giving a cheque to Eric Clarke, general secretary of the Scottish National Union of Mineworkers, in support of striking miners, 1984.

Left: Maria and her friend, Mora Carty, in Bundoran.

Maria and her sons, Chris and Stephen, on holiday in East Neuk.

With female anti-nuclear weapons campaigners from Glasgow at Greenham Common, 1981.

From left to right: Johann Lamont, Christine Hamilton, Maria Fyfe and Ian Davidson. The Scottish Labour Party Conference when Maria was elected to Scottish Executive of the Labour Party.

Maria and Jim Fyfe (behind the mother and toddler) in the crowd looking down on the Queen's Park bandstand, just before the Gaitskell furore erupted, 1962. The toddler is Robert (Bobby) Gillespie of Primal Scream fame with his mother Wilma.

Mary Barbour doing her bit to fight coronavirus, October 2020.
Credit: Colin Quigley, Govan Reminiscence Group

Chapter 8

'Heigh-Ho, Heigh-Ho,
It's Off to Work We Go'

WHEN IT CAME time to leave school my teachers thought there were scarcely more than two paths worth considering. University was one – and by that they meant Glasgow University. Most of its students were home grown and went back every night to their parents' houses when classes were over. No one left home to study. Indeed, it was seen as downright dubious especially for a girl to go away to study when there was a perfectly good, ancient university and with a worldwide reputation at that, on the doorstep. One girl dreamed of a life in Paris, debating philosophy over strong black coffee in a bistro on the Left Bank near the Sorbonne, but this was dismissed as a tiresome flight of fancy not worth taking seriously.

The other prospect held out to us was Notre Dame teacher training college, where students did a three year diploma course to qualify as a primary teacher. Students at the college had to board there, and the curfew hour left little room for social life outside. At least at the university they let you out of their sight, and when the day's classes were over were perfectly happy not to see you until the following morning.

As far as I was concerned university was out. I had been bored with schoolwork and did not want more of the same. I felt depressed to think that these were, as I was frequently told, the happiest days of my life. Would life really never get any better than this?

I was vaguely aware that people did study other things, like law and politics, but at that age nothing of that kind appealed. As for the training college, no, no, a thousand times no. The tyranny imposed by the nuns was bad enough, but what was worse was that these grown young women meekly accepted it.

So my pal Betty and I decided to do a business studies course at the Scottish College of Commerce in Pitt Street. We were the first from our school to exercise what they regarded as an exotic choice. Off we went to put our minds to the mysteries of economics, commerce, accountancy and shorthand and typing. It was not long before I realised I did not want to spend my life teaching the last two subjects. Can you imagine the boredom of standing before a shorthand class, day in, day out, reciting, 'pi, bi, ti, di, chi, ji,' relieved only by shouting above the clatter of 20 manual typewriters, 'f-t-f, f-r-f, f-g-f, f-v-f,' and so interminably on until the class were able to touch type 'the quick brown fox jumped over the lazy dog' at 40 words per minute? Mind you, these are skills I am glad to have, so I'm grateful that somebody had more patience than I had.

My dad would not let me take the first job I successfully applied for, secretary to a man with a fur coat business. The wage was too low, at £3 15s a week, and he wasn't having me educated to work for pay like that. So I had to phone the furrier and tell him I would not be starting after all, and as I put the phone down I felt worried in case I wouldn't get another job. But only a week later I was offered something far more satisfactory: secretary/shorthand typist to Sidney Harrison, the editor of the *Scottish Field*, for a salary of £4 10s a week. I was totally ignorant of rural affairs and country sports, but if it didn't matter to him it certainly didn't to me, and I hoped it would open up the doors of journalism for me. I was still daydreaming about becoming a reporter and had honed my shorthand skills with that in mind. I could now write Pitman at 140 words a minute. In those days the very few women on newspaper editorial staffs did the three 'effs' – food, furnishings and fashion. It was unheard of for women to do news reporting, and for years to come the only columnists writing on political or economic issues were men. I knew even less about fashion than I did about fishing, but I had a few pieces published by *The Glasgow Herald* and the *Evening Times* before boredom set in. I thought I'd rather not be a journalist than have to write this mind-numbing stuff about skirt lengths and necklines.

Emilio Coia, the cartoonist, was to be seen regularly around the office, contributing to the Outram & Company's wide variety of publications, and one day he pointed out to me something I had simply not noticed. In the entire Mitchell Street building, housing *The Glasgow Herald*, the *Bulletin*, the *Evening Times* and several magazines including the *Scottish Field*, he and I were the only Catholics. It says something for Sidney Harrison, who must have been aware of the prevailing attitude, that he flew in the face of it. All he cared about was competence and speed of delivery, and you could be a Zoroastrian for all it mattered to him.

He certainly cared about shorthand and typing skills. He had been a court reporter in his younger days, when it was essential to be able to note down verbatim every word that a witness said in the days before reporters started using tape recorders. He could read my Pitman shorthand upside down as he dictated at his normal talking speed while I sat opposite scribbling for dear life on my pad and tell me if I was doing an outline wrongly.

He had a ferocious temper, worsened every month as the publication deadline drew near. One of my first jobs was to organise his features cupboard for him, a simple task of filing contributions by regular writers and freelancers alike, so that they could be found quickly and thus reduce his blood pressure on that score at least. But one day he asked me to drop everything and fetch an article by Hugh MacDiarmid. I confidently opened up the cupboard, expecting to lay my hands on it at once. It was not to be seen. 'Where is it, where is it!' he cried, pacing up and down. 'I need it now.' I went through the entire collection from top to bottom, thinking it must have been misfiled accidentally. Still no sign of it. By this time Harrison was tearing his hair out. 'I'll look for it,' he growled, and immediately fished out a piece by somebody called Christopher Murray Grieve. 'You didn't know that was the same person!' he exclaimed. 'What do they teach you in school these days?' I just wondered why anyone who wasn't a criminal needed two names when one served most people well enough. As for all that Lallans – the supposed speech of the Lowland Scot in which MacDiarmid wrote, but no one I knew actually uttered – well, it was almost like learning another language. There is standard English, there is Glaswegian, and there are numerous other local dialects from the Shetlands to the Solway Firth, but there are not many Scots who can read MacDiarmid without the benefit of a glossary.

Working for Harrison was enjoyable. Apart from the business of getting together a magazine for publication, we received letters from all over the globe from people who wanted to know more about Scotland or trace their ancestors. Every month we published a selection of wedding pictures, and so many were sent in that choices had to be made and many rejected. That was one of my regular tasks. Mora's brother Eddie asked me why some of the ones we published were so unattractive. He remembers my answering, 'You should see the ones we don't publish.'

In the winter Harrison's red-coated pet Cocker Spaniel would lie across my feet as I sat at my typewriter, providing some extra warmth. The management of Outrams were a right bunch of skinflints. When my ancient typewriter gave up the ghost after its umpteenth repair, I pointed out the necessity of getting a new one, but they took so long to get around to it that, to get the work done, I brought in my own portable one. The managing director dropped in one day with a few visitors and seeing me tapping away at my dinky wee machine, he jovially remarked, 'Got your new typewriter, I see.' An instant decision had to be made. Should I pretend yes, this was it? I didn't want to embarrass him in front of his visitors. But then I might never get it and be left to use my less than sturdy machine that was little use for commercial purposes. 'No, I'm still waiting – this is my own,' I replied. This was clearly not the answer he wanted, but my new machine arrived a few days later.

After I was there about a year my dad asked if I was getting a raise. It hadn't even occurred to me to think about that. I plucked up my courage and asked Mr Harrison, who, while pointing out that I had still much to learn, was willing to support my request, which had to be sent to the headquarters in Perth. I was mad as hell when it came through – 5s. Then the much better paid editor of *Top Gear*, their motoring magazine, told me he had done the same, and got 5s.

I was one of the very few members of staff to join a trade union, the Clerical and Administrative Workers (CAWU), but the firm did not recognise it, so it could not bargain for me. I nevertheless stayed in membership for some years, and later Jim Fyfe, my boyfriend, also joined the CAWU. We regularly attended its branch meetings, and I was gratified when the members always agreed, without any debate, to anything I proposed in the way of motions, even ones criticising the union's national leadership. Further to that, my dad had a colleague who was in the same branch as me and commented to him 'That daughter of yours fairly has the gift of the gab.' Until one day some of the men spoke to Jim. 'Could you', they asked, 'persuade your girlfriend to give it a miss? We want to get a few drinks before the pub closes at nine o'clock.'

My next job was in the Scottish Gas Board, for a whole £7 a week. Imagine! I had decided that, if the kind of journalism I wanted to get a foothold on was not to be, then I may as well earn as much as I could in office work. My new job consisted of being secretary to three managers, and also supervisor of a small typing pool, in the Stores, Purchasing and Transport division which had an office in Milan Street on the south side. This looked as if it might be desperately dull compared to working on a magazine, but I thought I'd give it a go.

I was 19 or 20 at the time, and Edna Gracie, the most senior of the staff I had to supervise, was much older than me and fearsomely competent. She hadn't wanted the job I now had, preferring her own niche that suited her very well and paid for her holidays in Austria. Jean Butter could type up a storm and got through masses of work coming to us from not only the three bosses but the clerks downstairs as well. Later we acquired a junior called Monica, who was baffled by the posh English accent of the senior manager. On her first day at work, she was bade to enter his office, and he greeted her with the words, 'Now you're heah–'

'Whit's up w' ma hair?' she butted in. 'Dae ye no' like it this wey?'

He was somewhat taken aback by the egalitarianism of the workforce. The attitude of the blue collar workers in particular, he told me with some annoyance, was 'I'm as good as you are, and don't you forget it.' People interrupted him. They argued with him. They told him when they thought their way was a better way. I had to reassure him that this was just how it was in this part of the country – nothing personal. On my own first day at my new job I wore a fashionable blue sack dress. The next day I wore a green one. The only reason I remember anything this trivial is that it confused some fellow workers, for whom those colours were code for whether you were a Catholic or a Protestant. You might think the name, Maria O'Neill, would have given them a clue, but there you go.

I was not long there before I heard the office gossip. The top manager (allegedly, for the benefit of m'learned friends) had a mistress installed in a nearby flat. This was not simply her own flat, that happened to be near the office, the tale went. He was paying for it. She was a Kept Woman. But horror of horrors: I was told amid much chortling by the staff that I bore some resemblance to her. Same height and build, same complexion and colour of hair. This was embarrassing. Suppose people thought I was this immoral creature when I accompanied my boss outside the office? Tom Bucknall, one of the other senior men, hastened to reassure me. 'No one', he said, 'would think you were anyone's floozie. And for God's sake, don't tell him you know about her. He thinks nobody does.'

The senior boss was keen to get a better job, and every Monday morning, just about, I had to type up a different CV, doctored to suit the advertiser. I could read the job ads in the Sunday broadsheets and anticipate what he would go for. To advance his career he also thought it would help if he joined the Masons, and he undertook to get his Lodge's secret paperwork typed up at the office. The snag was, he could not ask a Catholic to do it. So he called in Jean whenever he needed a document prepared, and she would check the spelling of unfamiliar words with me before duly presenting the finished documents to him. Not once did he ever realise I was seeing them anyway. Edna refused to have anything to do with it.

He had some good points, though. He ran a Christmas party for the workforce's children, with a Santa's sack full of toys that it was not widely known he paid for himself. It was I who went shopping for them with a fistful of notes from his wallet. He organised a Driver of the Year competition, to encourage safe and skilful driving amongst the drivers of the 300-vehicle-fleet. We were the first nationalised industry in Scotland to do that.

He sometimes asked me for advice on problems that arose amongst the staff. There was the time a comptometer operator, a single woman in her late 20s, was very visibly pregnant. This was apparently the first time such a thing had happened amongst the staff. The mother of one of the other girls wrote an angry letter to him, pressing him to sack her, as she was a bad example to the younger ones. I couldn't believe that anyone could be so harsh, wanting someone to lose their income when a baby was on the way. In any case, I pointed out, far from being an influence on the other girls, they felt sorry for her. If anything, they thought her a bit simple for trusting a boyfriend that they had disliked. The boss agreed. He felt contempt for the kind of self-righteous person who could write such a letter. What he did then was dictate a letter to the other girl's mother, giving her a flea in her ear, which I thoroughly enjoyed typing up. It was to be years before the law was changed to prevent women from being dismissed on grounds of pregnancy, and by that time it was rightly considered completely irrelevant whether the mother to be was single or not.

Then I got promoted to a job with a more senior manager, the head of the Finance Department in the George Square office. Now I was the personal secretary to the one boss and had no supervisory tasks. So, less responsibility, but more money, simply because Mr Auld was higher up the pecking order. Not without objection from one of the Masons working in the office, who kept a tally of Catholics and Protestants being recruited and complained if the number of Tims was getting too high for his liking. The management, to their credit, completely ignored this.

One of my tasks was to phone all the local gas stations around the West of Scotland, to remind their engineers if they had not sent in their statistical returns on gas usage for the month, which I had to gather together into the one large document, to do so. One small office started sending in figures that neither matched their previous record, nor others of a similar size. When I phoned the engineer, he told me he was there on his own, the clerkess having left, and he was fed up waiting for her replacement who was not yet in post. But why, I asked, were the figures so out of kilter? 'Och,' he replied, 'she'd been sending in these figures for years and no one ever queried them. I haven't a clue how she got them, so I just put anything I thought seemed reasonable in the boxes to keep head office satisfied. I've got more to be going on with here than doing paperwork.' I've never really trusted statistical returns since.

My new boss was a kindly man. In those days it was common for people who hadn't paid their gas bill to be cut off, but he took account of hardship when he knew about it. I drew one particular case to his attention. Guy Aldred, a well-known figure in Glasgow politics, was an anarchist and publisher of a magazine called *The Word*, which he sent free every month to every Scottish Labour MP. His premises were a small shop in Montrose Street, where my boyfriend Jim and I often browsed amongst the books on sale. I knew that Guy was getting on in years, and lived on a pittance, so when I saw the shop's address on a list of business premises to have their gas cut off, I drew it to Mr Auld's attention. He immediately ordered the supply to continue, saying Guy – of whom he had never heard – was obviously not one of those people who could pay but wouldn't, and it would be a shame to load this worry onto him. Guy Aldred died the following year.

Mr Auld was a great friend of Harry Diamond, who later in his career became Glasgow City Council's press officer, and more famous than many of the councillors, but at that time was the gas board's publicity manager. I stood at Harry's desk one day, waiting to give him a message from my boss, while he was on the phone. I could clearly hear the voice at the other end. It was the *Evening Times*, asking if he could offer an explanation why a customer who had ordered a white, four burner, Cannon gas cooker had received, in turn, a white three burner, a cream three burner, then a cream four burner, all of which were standing at the back of her house, blocking her path, and getting rained on, while she awaited what she had actually ordered. 'Yes, of course I can offer you an explanation,' he said. 'Sheer fucking incompetence.'

By this time, I was a member of the National Association of Local Government Officers (NALGO), the trade union for office staff in local authorities and the public utilities. Like trade unions generally it was male dominated, and it never occurred to them that they might not be doing a decent job for their female members. In the gas industry the clerks, mostly male, were paid more than the secretaries all of whom were female although secretaries had to acquire extra skills to be able to do their job at all. So I argued we should be paid the same for equal levels of responsibility. 'Not at all', argued some of the clerks at our branch meeting. 'You only type. We do the job of working out what needs to be said.'

Well, there was an obvious answer to that. I got the secretaries and typists to meet together and we decided on a two-pronged attack. First, we would get a note into the hands of all the new female juniors coming in straight from school and advise them not to choose the secretarial ladder and pick the clerical one instead. This was vital, because we knew from our own experience that girls leaving school were constantly assured by career guidance advisers that secretarial skills would lead to a well-paid job, whereas the reality was they would do better as clerks: better paid from the outset, and with prospects of advancement far greater than secretaries could hope for.

But the second tactic had immediate effect. We decided we would type exactly what we had been given to type, whether handwritten or dictated. We would not correct grammar or spelling. Misplaced apostrophes would stay misplaced. If parts of addresses, or the date, were left out, they remained left out. Dictated letters would include every 'um' and 'err'. We would not turn the clerks', 'In reply to yours of 10th inst.' into, 'Thank you for your letter of 10th June.' For some reason office clerks throughout Britain spoke normal English, but wrote in commercialese, and it was the secretaries' task to modernise the gas industry's communications with the outside world. So we chortled amongst ourselves that day as we faithfully typed up the usual cliché-ridden verbiage. In short, we did not use our intelligence at all. On strike? Not us. We were doing exactly what we were told. I once met an old workmate who still recalled with glee the day we did that. She had been dining out on it all those years.

Our branch officers finally agreed to negotiate on our behalf. I sent a questionnaire around all the female staff. From this it transpired that women supervising large typing pools were paid no more than a basic grade clerk who had no supervisory role at all. We discovered that Home Service advisers, who had to spend two years in full time education to gain their diploma, were paid the same as a male clerk without any further education.

Annoyingly enough the successful outcome, creating equal pay in 1964, came too late for me to benefit. I had to leave the gas board because the rules under which Jim would be entitled to a student grant when we got married meant I couldn't be in regular paid work.

There was no women's movement astir at the time, but there had been equal pay disputes here and there, most notably in Rolls-Royce where Agnes McLean led the women on the shop floor to success in the 1940s. These young secretaries and typists where I worked were nobody's idea of trade union militants, but they knew when they were being treated unfairly and were prepared to do something about it in an age when they had the whip hand, for jobs were plentiful and the employers knew it. When my dad heard what I had been up to, he remarked, 'Just like your grandfather.' That was something I was proud to hear.

But equal pay was not the only problem. I found that, although I had been doing some of an older clerk's work while he was off sick for several months, when he took early retirement I was not even allowed to apply for his job because I was on the secretarial pay scale, which was totally separate from the clerical scale, and never the twain should meet. And that was not all.

The gas board had some attractive houses for let to their employees, and my boyfriend Jim and I were looking for accommodation at a cheap rent for when we got married. One such house, a cottage near one of their gasholders, would have suited admirably. I was told they were only let to male employees, as women left when they had children. In vain did I point out that men left too, to advance their careers, and hadn't they noticed not all their women employees had left when they had children anyway? But logic had nothing to do with it. They would not budge. So the gas industry is to blame for my becoming a feminist. Although we still have a road to travel, take note that all these discriminatory practices would now be illegal.

All the office staff went on strike one day, and by lunchtime we had won our case. The action was in defence of a clerk in the sales department, who had been sacked for throwing a teacup (empty at the time, mind you) at his supervisor. Now, no one was saying this was acceptable behaviour. But we learned that his supervisor had been constantly needling him, and making his life a misery, because he was gay. Added to that, one of the senior management had been found guilty of driving while drunk when on gas board business, and he was not sacked. We all felt it was simply unfair. So we argued our colleague should be allowed to transfer to another section, and the management accepted this. That was my only experience of being on strike while I worked there.

Jim and I got married in 1964, and started learning to live, not on two wages, but on his married student's grant topped up by our casual earnings. Looking back on it, I deplore the fact we were so reckless as to have two children born in quick succession, in the following two years, while he was still a student, instead of waiting until we had a decent income coming in. We were young and full of confidence in our ability to cope. Mum would have said it was sinful to take precautions anyway, and Dad said, 'You can't put an old head on young shoulders.' I heard that remark quite often.

When our sons Stephen and Christopher were infants I had occasional bouts of casual work, while Jim studied for his degree in social sciences. I did secretarial work at a family firm of pump manufacturers in Govan called Dawson and Downie, and although they were highly regarded by their customers for the quality of their merchandise, they knew nothing of marketing. One day I opened a letter from an American client, who asked – and you could sense the exasperation in every line – 'Why don't you sell yourselves? You sit like clams on the beach, waiting for what the tide washes up!'

There was another secretary in a permanent job there, who was a member of the Communist Party, and at tea breaks Cathy and I would debate politics. In both our minds, just about everything was political anyway. In line with her party's longstanding sensible advice to its members, she made sure her performance at work was always blameless. Competent and calm. Never late for work, never the first out the door when the day's work was over. Taking a 'sickie' was something she would never have contemplated. The idea being, that this way you earn the esteem of your fellow workers, and when issues need to be discussed you get listened to with respect, and not ignored as too lazy or incompetent to be worth hearing. So, when a vacancy arose, the boss called her in and asked her if she knew any other Communist secretaries, as he could do with more workers like her.

I had enjoyed my time there, so when I was next looking for a few months' work I phoned them up. I had originally gone to them through an agency, which paid buttons to the temps, so I pointed out that they could save the agency fee, which was a lot higher than the normal wage. The boss wondered if that was maybe a bit unethical. He had only got my services originally because of the agency. Could I, he asked, sign up with the agency again, and he would ask them to send me? I pointed out that, one, I was not enslaved to the agency, two, like Eliza Doolittle's dad, I couldn't afford morals like these. We came to an agreement, and Cathy and I resumed solving the world's problems over our cups of tea.

Then I spent a short while in the office at Singer's sewing machine factory in Clydebank, a huge plant employing thousands. They knew all about spinning before the words 'spin doctor' were ever heard. Extolling the virtues of your product is one thing. Lying to your employees is another. They had a glossy newsletter exhorting us all to be mindful that we were facing competition from the Far East, where pay was so much lower, so our pay claims had to be moderated. The deceit in this message was that Singers themselves had set up no fewer than 13 factories throughout the Far East, two of which were in Japan. Their net sales for the Far East alone in 1963 amounted to over $73 million. So I pointed this out in a letter to the *Clydebank Post*. As their ads said, 'Singer has the world sewn up'. I later found out I had been blacklisted, as was only to be expected, but as I had decided to study for university entrance it didn't matter to me. I wouldn't be applying for any job until I graduated, and then my employer would probably be a local education department, none of which were likely to subscribe to blacklisting organisations. I didn't guess for a moment that this would matter 20 years later, when I was seeking selection as Labour's candidate for the constituency of Glasgow Maryhill in the forthcoming General Election. Nor did I foresee the time would come when I would be doing my bit to destroy the best known blacklisting organisation in British industry – the Economic League. (This story is told in *A Problem Like Maria*.)

Chapter 9

'It's My Party'

IF YOUR IDEA of a good way to spend a summer Sunday evening is to stand on a soapbox in Glasgow's Sauchiehall Street, enlightening the pedestrians about the affairs of the world, you would have enjoyed being in the Labour Party's Young Socialists. We were convinced we had the right line on every current issue, and many an esoteric one as well. At least it gave us practice in public speaking without the benefit of a microphone and dealing with hecklers. My friend Margie was our YS treasurer, and before we could even enter the hall for our meeting we had to have a whip round for the 15s that would allow us to obtain the key. If we couldn't gather that sum we just went to somebody's house, or to the local café where we were allowed to spin out just one soft drink all night.

Our YS branch won the Labour Party's national under-25s public speaking competition. My own contribution to this success was the modest one of chairing our session, having assiduously studied the National Council of Labour Colleges' course on chairing meetings, and read Walter Citrine's *ABC of Chairmanship*. I wouldn't have dared to attempt chairing a meeting without boning up on the rules, but I have often sat these many years through meetings that got into confusion because the person in the Chair had felt no need to do so.I had joined the Labour Party in 1960, the year after they had lost three General Elections in a row. The media were saying that Labour was all washed up. I had bought my first political paperback, *Must Labour Lose?*, a Penguin Special by Mark Abrams and others, and felt troubled by what I read. It seemed Labour was doomed to perpetual opposition.

My whole life and family history fed into my concern that La-bour might not ever form a government again: Dad's loss of oppor-tunity when a schoolboy, both my parents' educations – such as they were – ending at the age of 14, the cost of healthcare denying treatment to working class families before the NHS was created by Aneurin Bevan, my dad's years on the dole, the imbalance in power between employer and employee. Although our family had been fortunate where housing was concerned, I was well aware of home-lessness and poor housing conditions. All bread and butter domes-tic issues, but absolutely crucial for the achievement of anything like a more equal society.

My brother Joe and I, along with some of my pals, decided to knock on the door of the local Labour rooms in Craigton and ask if they needed any help, without having the least idea what we might be able to do. All we knew was that Labour was continuing to lose and yet more Tory rule was simply unthinkable. We were welcomed with open arms when they saw before them young, ener-getic, enthusiastic people who weren't Trotskyists. Being under 25, I was eligible for the newly recreated youth wing.

We hadn't even heard of Leon Trotsky. I simply wanted to help Labour back into power, and even when I got to hear of that par-ticular Russian revolutionary, which wasn't long, I was puzzled about why the views of a long dead Bolshevik were considered sig-nificant by people living in Britain now. Even less did I understand why and how this tiny sect managed to split up into even tinier fac-tions. We were told that the Labour Party had disbanded its earlier youth organisation, the League of Youth, on account of Trotskyist infiltration, but had decided to give it another go under the name of the Young Socialists.

These factions had not gone away. The Labour Party tried to defend itself by creating a list of proscribed organisations, and if memory serves me there were over 20 such bodies, membership of which was incompatible with carrying a Labour card. The list included any political party that stood candidates against Labour ones in elections, reasonably enough. Then there were all the many Trotskyist factions, which practised 'entryism' on the grounds that, as the working class looked to Labour, that was the obvious place to be to wean people away from false consciousness and attract them to their brand, as opposed to all other competing brands, of socialist enlightenment. All this served only to whet my curiosity. What, I wondered, did these organisations have to say for themselves, and what did they do or say that was so dangerous?

I was persuaded to go along to a few meetings of one such group, the International Socialists, which later became the Socialist Workers' Party. Their leading theoretician, Tony Cliff, argued that the Soviet Union was not just a 'deformed' workers' state, as other Trotskyists argued, but was in reality 'state capitalist'. This, I gathered, meant that just as capitalists vied with one another to gain monopoly, the state in Russia enjoyed its own monopoly status. That made some people feel even more left-wing.

A lot of my new friends were in that group, but I found it much too domineering. One night one of the comrades took me to task about a few articles I had written for the *Glasgow Evening Times* on light-hearted subjects and berated me for using my skills so frivolously. 'You should,' he thundered at me, 'use your abilities to help the cause.' I was very willing to help Socialism along in any way I could, but not to be told how to use my spare time. Some while later one of my friends, John Culbert, a member of that organisation, won a car in a competition, and they demanded that he handed it over to them. He refused to do that, but he did let them borrow it whenever they wanted, and he paid for the petrol. Another Trot group was the Socialist Labour League (SLL), which published a paper aimed at young left-wingers, called 'Keep Left', edited by one Roger Protz.

For a while the SLL dominated the Labour youth scene. When I say 'dominated' I merely mean that they were foremost in offering food for thought to young people wholly ignorant of political theory, but who had intellectual curiosity and enjoyed exploring political ideas. They didn't even try to recruit all that hard. They didn't capture branches or winkle its members into positions of authority. Chic McCafferty was their leading light in our YS branch, and impressed all the new members with his comprehensive knowledge of theoretical matters. In later life he dropped Trotskyism and became a highly regarded mainstream Labour Left councillor and deputy leader. This may have had something to do with my friend Margie McGowan, who, although she became his wife, remained resolutely unimpressed by all this theoretical wrangling over matters that didn't have anything practical to offer. She became a councillor too. Sadly, Chic died some years ago, robbing them of the retirement years they had hoped to enjoy together, and Margie herself died more recently.

Then there was the International Marxist Group (IMG), who seemed largely to consist of middle class students. Their female members at one stage felt the need to discuss issues of particular relevance to women, but wanted to do so without the men present, as they talked too much and too forcefully, and it was necessary to encourage quieter, newer women members to speak up. This upset their more supportive male colleagues, who protested that they wanted to be helpful and thought it wrong to be excluded. At this point any savvy young woman might wonder about ulterior motives for all this enthusiasm for yet more meetings they could so easily avoid. It has to be said this behaviour displayed by the women members sits oddly with the recollections of some erstwhile members of days in their youth when they slept in comrades' flats when attending meetings down south. They were amazed when waking up in the morning at the sight of IMG women walking around unconcernedly in their undies as they headed for the shower or stood at the cooker frying eggs. The working class girls they knew in Glasgow would never do that.But how to overcome the dilemma of male attendance or absence at these women's issues meetings? A motion was put to the meeting that the men who wanted to, should be allowed to sit in, but only if they kept quiet and covered their heads with paper bags, lest any eyebrow lifting, nose wrinkling, or sarcastic grin indicated a point of view. I understand they were not quite mad enough to adopt this solution.

A breakaway group of former IMG members, seeing themselves as the really serious foes of the British state, unlike their parent organisation and all their would-be competitors, therefore reasoned that each one of them needed an alias to make the state's task of re-pressing them more difficult. They could get pretty upset if anyone so forgot themselves as to address them by their real name. *Life of Brian* had it spot on.

IMG members and their competitors would move from bedsit to bedsit, so they could join Labour Party branches and put their arguments to them, capture positions like, er, Minute Secretary, and join in the infighting with the other Trots. Like all other Trot groups I have ever known, their tactic was to never find anything done by a Labour Government or council any good. They would scornfully demand more, even when it was obvious it was not achievable at present or in the foreseeable future. This was not mere cussedness. It was born out of theory. Revolutionaries were to make 'transitional demands' on Labour governments on the way to achieving their own version of Utopia. Lenin himself, who wrote an interesting short work entitled *Left Wing Communism: An Infantile Disorder* pointed out that it was necessary to take the people with you, and not get so far ahead you had lost touch with them. Then we had the comical outcome, election after election, of Labour candidates in working class areas winning huge majorities, while those sects who fancied themselves as being the true leaders of the working class, realising they could win only a derisory vote, would end up calling on their readers to support us, 'critically', after attacking us week in week out since the previous election. Pat Fryd and Tony Southall were the leading lights in the IMG and held meetings in their home in Glasgow on Sunday mornings. You might think getting out of bed and putting on the kettle for those arriving would be a basic courtesy. But no. They sat up, pillows propped behind them, still in their pyjamas, while other members pulled up chairs and sat around the bed. When Jim Mackechnie (another who, after a short time, grew out of this and later became a vigorous and committed Labour councillor) objected that if he could get out of bed, shower, dress, and travel from Edinburgh by train to their home, the least they could do was get out of bed, he was told not to be so bourgeois.

Neither the SLL, the International Socialists, nor the IMG were anything like as invasive as the Revolutionary Socialist League (RSL) was later to be. Never heard of it? Not surprising. In the '50s and '60s the RSL survived the Labour Party's efforts to rid itself of such influences, because it was so small and insignificant it escaped attention. If you were in any such group – or 'tendency' as the RSL liked to call themselves – you spent your time learning up the line on arcane points of doctrine. And there was the problem of whether there could be Socialism in one country, or did it need worldwide revolution. With youthful optimism I thought I might see it in Britain before too long. But if it needed worldwide success, hang on, wait a minute. Did that mean we had to wait for religious fundamentalists in ill-educated countries, South American tribes who barely knew there was a world outside their part of the Amazon, not to mention Americans who thought our National Health Service was Communism? Trotsky had written books on such subjects, as had the leading lights of the various Trot groups, which we were earnestly advised to read. I did try, I really did.

But I have to admit I was equally baffled by a mantra much favoured by people who were decidedly not Trots, but Labour Party socialists, when they were concluding speeches. Especially if they were seeking election for something. They would often quote the words of Aneurin Bevan: 'The religion of Socialism is the language of priorities.' But surely everyone, regardless of their political views, had priorities? Only later did I learn the context in which Bevan had spoken these words. When the 1945 Labour Government had delivered on healthcare, nationalised the coal industry and freed the working class from fear of hunger, basic aims had been achieved. Now it was a matter of choices. He put it to a meeting of the Fabians that the good life would be impossible until we have produced a citizenry that is capable not only of selections but of rejections. In other words, don't just keep on drawing up wish lists, as we tend to be prone to do. Decide what really matters and go for it with all the determination you can muster.I was only a member of the Labour Party for a year or so when I was elected Secretary of the Constituency Labour Party in Craigton. This came about, not because of any political precocity on my part, but just because of my inoffensiveness. The previous Secretary, Isabel Clark, a woman strongly committed to the Campaign for Democratic Socialism, a right-wing Gaitskellite group that had recently been formed, made a habit of reading out correspondence from bodies of whom she disapproved with a sneering air, and the contrast was marked when her whole demeanour and tone of voice indicated when she approved of anything she was reading aloud. I was actually quite friendly with Isabel for a while, but realised I was never going to be a soul mate of someone whose idea of a good time was to sit through hours and hours of Wagner at the Bayreuth Festival.

One night she was away, and I was asked to do her secretarial duties. I did it as I thought best. I gave them the gist of what each letter said, rather than read it all out word for word, which saved a lot of the meeting's time, and I adopted the same carefully neutral tone for all of them. Everyone said afterwards what a pleasant change it was to have a meeting not put in a bad mood before we even started debating anything. Bad moods and endless bickering were a common experience, I was to find, as the constituency party was constantly at loggerheads with one of the branches, not over anything political, but about who was responsible for the financial affairs of the hall that had been recently built. Somehow those concerned with getting the hall built had contrived to be unclear about who exactly was responsible for paying off the debt. It was not appreciated when I said we had a long way to go in organising a socialist society when we could not even get a wee hall built without a row. At the next AGM, to my surprise, I was nominated for Secretary, and was elected 'nem. con.'. Thus, began a lifetime of being Secretary, Chair, Treasurer, Political Education Officer, Fund Raising Officer, you name it. I even told fortunes at our fête, dressed up as a gypsy. Knowing nothing about reading palms, I learned from a book on palmistry borrowed from the library that amongst all the tosh about head and heart lines there were some real clues to tell you things about people. Doctors do it as a matter of course. How does a person walk and sit down? 'Ridges and white marks on the fingernails give clues about a person's health. Smooth hands indicate not much rough work.'

I found to my amazement that people I had believed were sensible actually thought I had mystical powers, because I told them things they thought I could not have known. One middle aged woman trudged into the tent, plonked herself down heavily, and told me she was worried about something and she was hoping I could help. I replied, 'You're worried about your family, aren't you?' Did you ever know any middle aged mother who never worried about her family? We talked about her teenage son's inadequacies, and I gave her common sense advice she could probably have worked out perfectly well for herself. In case anyone is harbouring a belief that I do have psychic gifts, but am perversely denying it, let me reveal that I also told Hugh Gaitskell his fortune when he was brought through my tent flap by a party official. I was no fan of the party leader over his hostility to us ban-the-bombers, but for the benefit of the *Sunday Express* photographer I foretold he would lead the party to victory and live a long and happy life. He died soon after.

If I thought the party bureaucracy would try to educate and inform its young members I was wrong. Apart from the annual weekend school at the Rob Roy Hotel near Aberfoyle in the Trossachs, on one occasion addressed by Denis Healey who was sent to persuade us of the multilateralist case, there was no organised effort to advance our political education and knowledge of Democratic Socialism.

What they did do soon became a matter of annoyance to me. Willie Marshall, the Scottish General Secretary, paid a lot of attention to the members of Glasgow University Labour Club, some of whom were also stars of the student debating society. Among them there were, admittedly, names that were to become famous, like Jimmy Gordon who set up Radio Clyde. Donald Dewar and John Smith were leading lights, and in those days I disliked them both. John was in the thick of a right-wing plot to try to prevent my fellow left-winger, friend and workmate Neil Carmichael from being the Labour candidate for Woodside in the 1962 by-election brought about by the resignation of the sitting Conservative MP. John's preferred candidate was Arthur Houston, a fellow Gaitskellite and former star of the Glasgow University Labour Club. In those days the rules for eligibility to vote in candidate selection were a lot slacker, and John took advantage of the leeway it created in a way that he later on, to his credit, felt shamefaced about. John, a lawyer, not a boilermaker, voted as a member of a defunct branch of the General and Municipal Workers' Union (GMWU) that had not met for two years.

Although the Gaitskellites didn't succeed, their behaviour rankled. Donald hadn't really done anything personally to offend, other than having views more right-wing than my own. He came as a speaker to our YS branch one night, and we sat there thinking up difficult questions, just for badness. I was mad as hell, because it was assumed by Marshall that just because they were students they were more worthy of the party's attention. I wonder if he ever realised how mistaken he was in ignoring the talent to be found in the YS, for in the youth wing of those days there were many members who demonstrated their abilities by going from working class childhoods in the housing schemes and the tenement streets into highly successful careers, and one or two who rose spectacularly, like Gus Macdonald, who began his working life as an apprentice in the shipyards and rose to become a TV tycoon – and a member of the House of Lords – from the modest start in the media world of working in the circulation department of *Tribune*. From among my friends in our YS branch alone there emerged in due course no fewer than five councillors, along with Morag Alexander who went on to head up the Equal Opportunities Commission in Scotland, and Ken Munro who became the head of representation in Scotland of the European Commission. Our branch was not unusual. Other young recruits to the party around the city at that time went on to be successful in pursuits as diverse as the Carnaby Street fashion trade, trade unionism, social work, education and industry. But none of this talent was recognised by the party's organisers.

They didn't expect any of us – Young Socialists or student debaters – to raise awkward questions. The students they saw as future candidates for Parliament. The YS were merely a source of youthful energy for climbing stairs and leafleting.

When, more than two decades later, I was elected to Parliament,

Donald and John had changed and so had I. I didn't expect John to agree with me one night when we were talking about the state of affairs in Liverpool. I argued Militant would not have been able to take control of the party in that city if it had not been for the atrocious behaviour of their right-wing predecessors, who had made the Labour Party's name mud. To my surprise he was of the same opinion. As for Donald, we became allies when coping with the more nationalist tendencies in our ranks, and we laughed about our memories of our time in the youth wing. He admitted I had every right to be annoyed at such elitist behaviour from party apparatchiks.

I didn't like the idea of student debating when I first came across John and Donald, where a much admired skill lay in the ability to argue a case that you didn't actually believe in. No doubt a highly useful accomplishment for a future career in the courtrooms, but it gave me a lifelong scepticism about speechmaking, and I would look for proof of sincerity in actions, not just words. I found it more interesting to talk with young men who didn't indulge in the artificial skills of debating but proclaimed themselves revolutionaries.

'But how do you want to overthrow the capitalist state?' I asked Chic nervously. 'With bombs?'

'No, of course not,' he replied. 'We aren't terrorists.'

Phew. 'So how then?'

'The class war. Educate, agitate, organise. For example, workers need to understand the concept of surplus value to realise how they are exploited under capitalism. We need to agitate to rouse workers to improve their wages and conditions, and seek not just improvements in society, but a new society that will arise out of the ashes of capitalism. And of course, the need for organisation hardly needs explaining.'

That meant there was much to learn. As it turned out, the YS couldn't even organise a bus run, having failed to collect all the fares and much to their annoyance put the party in debt to the coach company. We were nearly disbanded for financial incompetence, but the Co-op women demanded we be given another chance.

While the adult party failed to teach us anything, and spent its time worrying about tiny Trot sects, it spent years not facing up to the infiltration by the most damaging of all those factions, the RSL, which had been germinating quietly and unnoticed when other Trot groups held their attention. In Liverpool, as elsewhere, they told everyone they were simply Labour Party members who read *Militant*. The editors of Militant always publicly denied the very existence of the RSL.

At the time I was in the YS no Trot faction had any power anywhere. That is, unless you count Harry Selby, his wife Jean, and son Leon, all of whom succeeded in getting themselves elected as Labour councillors. Harry was, and his family too, I expect, a member of an obscure organisation known as the Left Fraction of the Fourth International, while maintaining membership of the Labour Party. Indeed, he was appointed as the Fraction's representative in Scotland. He and his family members achieved selection as Labour candidates for safe council seats because they were members of a very small party branch. History does not record any upswing in revolutionary fervour amongst the Glasgow councillors as a result of their presence. Later, in 1974, Harry was elected MP for Glasgow Govan, where he stayed until a coup in the local party ousted him five years afterwards.

However, Harry can be credited with recruiting into the Labour Party some of the lively young men who had been involved when the apprentices in engineering and shipbuilding went on strike in 1960 for higher pay. Among them was Gus Macdonald, who chaired the Clydeside Junior Workers' Committee. Some names that were later to become famous were involved in the apprentices' action: Billy Connolly, Alex Ferguson and Jimmy Reid, who was at that time a member of the Communist Party all played a role, although others, notably Jimmy Airlie, did most of the work.

The Communist Party had been highly active in support of the apprentices, the Young Communist League playing a leading role, and as a result new members were rolling in. But some other lads were doubtful. They knew that their Catholic parents would crack up if they did any such thing. One of the apprentices, Jimmy

O'Neill, was Harry's nephew, and Harry mentioned to him that the Labour Party had just newly created an organisation for young people, called the Young Socialists. This seemed just the ticket, and so a number of bright young people were recruited to Labour, and spent their formative political years hearing the views of all sorts of weird and wonderful groups, for want of an educational programme in the party they had joined.

Apprentices and office workers, bus drivers and nurses, we all entered into the same debates. Meanwhile the male working class were going in their tens of thousands to the football, and the women to the new entertainment – bingo – of which some of our members disapproved strongly on the grounds that women, as keepers of the household purse, should not engage in any form of gambling. Both the women and the men generally showed a deplorable lack of interest in their own emancipation. If, as Marx and Engels apparently said, 'the emancipation of the workers must be the act of the working class itself' then when were they going get on with it?

But we didn't just earnestly debate. At our parties we sang songs I'd never heard before. There were all the new anti-bomb songs, like 'Ding Dong Dollar', to the tune of 'Ye Canny Shove Yer Granny Aff a Bus', a song that every Glaswegian child knows. That was when I learned the words of the 'Red Flag' and 'The Internationale'. I have never stopped loving both of these anthems, but I can never hear 'The Internationale' sung without thinking of when my five year old son Stephen, at a May Day rally, asked me why they were all singing about starlings.

'Eh?'

'They're singing "Arise ye starlings from your slumbers."'

There were few older members who took any interest in our political development: Neil and Kay Carmichael and Norman and Janey Buchan were outstanding exceptions. The Carmichaels hosted parties in their house in Partickhill Road, where we danced, sang, drank, sang, ate, sang and ended up debating political issues well into the small hours. The Buchans's house in Peel Street was an open house to the young members. Their generosity with their time was astonishing. They educated us, and made politics seem fun. It was through the Buchans that we became involved in the burgeoning Glasgow folk music scene, when many a cellar and attic that should have been condemned was pressed into service for folk concerts. That was when we learned the songs of the Labour movement, Irish rebel songs, traditional songs handed down for generations and the peace songs that were being written by the score as Polaris came up the Clyde. I cannot exaggerate how much our generation of young politicos owes to them.

Chapter 10

'H-Bomb's Thunder'

THE CND WAS NOT hard to notice. The black plastic badge with the peace sign in white was something new on the streets. I was not convinced at first of the case for unilateral nuclear disarmament. Then I read Bertrand Russell's *Has Man a Future?*.

So I was not one of the first to sit down at Ardnadam Pier, protesting against the Polaris missiles being brought to the Holy Loch in March 1961, but the following year I joined in a sit-down at Faslane and waited, limbs hanging loose so as to be as dead weight as possible, and not resisting arrest, to be lifted by the police. I was duly hauled, along with Jim and some of our friends, into a Black Maria. But, we wondered, why had the policemen left the door of the vehicle open? Were the plods really that stupid?

We had good cause to be puzzled. Demonstrations were banned under the Public Order Act, a law that had been introduced in the 1930s to deal with fascism. In February six members of the Committee of 100, an organisation set up by Russell to oppose the bomb by civil disobedience tactics, had been tried at the Old Bailey for conspiracy, having organised a demonstration at the Wethersfield RAF base in Essex. They were sentenced to 18 months in prison for each man, and 12 months for the one woman.

After some anxious gazing to left and right, we hastily made our escape. Why were we so fortunate? I don't know. Maybe the authorities had taken note of the public outrage at the harsh treatment of people who had been peacefully demonstrating. Maybe the Glasgow polis's attitude was different from their counterparts in Essex, and they had just not wanted the bother of arresting us when we had done no damage, and no one was hurt. Or maybe some retired former senior policeman looks back with a chuckle at the time he and his mates made such a bloomer.

I had met Jim for the first time on an Anti-Apartheid demonstration in freezing February weather, the hailstones bouncing off us. He was looking utterly miserable. But I liked the look of this tall, lean, dark-haired fellow, with a copy of *Tribune*, the left-wing Labour weekly, sticking out of his duffle coat pocket.

A mutual friend told me he had just got out of bed after having pleurisy. I, like the good socialist I tried to be, thought his need was greater than mine. I offered to lend him my suede mittens, which he refused, but from then on we seemed to keep bumping into each other. Later on, he confessed that our being at the same meetings and poster painting sessions was no accident. As a boyfriend he was different from previous ones. He read widely and questioned deeply. No 'learning up the line' for him. He read political theory and his jackets were endearingly ruined by having their pockets stuffed with books and newspapers. He talked to me like a human being with a brain and didn't chat me up.

Jim and I went on Aldermaston marches at Easter, sleeping overnight in school halls and large circus tents. We would assemble at Aldermaston, Britain's nuclear bomb factory, and walk all the way to London. There were thousands of people on those marches, from all over Britain and other countries. It was sore on feet unaccustomed to walking more than a few hundred yards, but we applied surgical spirit to our soles and kept our spirits up by singing as we marched along. We had plenty of songs to sing. 'I Shall Not Be Moved', 'The H-Bomb's Thunder', and for laughs, 'The Misguided Missile and the Misguided Miss'. Josh Macrae had a basement in Balgrayhill that was a magnet for folkies, attracting Morris Blythman aka Thurso Berwick, Bobby Campbell, Hamish Imlach, Sean Tierney and Matt McGinn. On the bus going down to Aldermaston, Matt would keep us entertained, singing one rousing song after another, and sometime one of his own compositions, like:

There's a fellow down the road that I avoid.
He's one of them they call the unemployed.
He says it's all because of me,
He can't get a job when I've got three:
I've three nights and a Sunday double time.

The Labour Party in Glasgow was deeply divided over nuclear weapons and the siting of Polaris on the Holy Loch. Some, usually older members, simply trusted their leader to be all-wise and all-knowing. They argued he had access to information the general public did not have, and so was in a position to make such a decision that we were not. Some believed in deterrence to avoid destruction by a hostile power. Another argument was that Britain had to keep its status as a major power, and a ticket to the top table meant being a nuclear power. The rest of us were angered by the millions squandered on nuclear weaponry when there were so many better things to spend it on, and we did not trust anyone's finger on the button. The prospect of nuclear war seemed very real.

The Conservative government of the time told a blatant lie: that Polaris had to be sited on the Holy Loch, where admittedly there were so many people living close by, because the surrounding hills made it hugely difficult for any airborne attacker to approach. We must have been pretty naive to believe that was their reason. No one would develop any missile, at such vast expense, that depended on such specific physical surroundings. Incredibly, a similar argument is advanced today, that if some future independent Scotland's government removes Trident from the Clyde then Britain will be rid of it altogether, as there are no waters deep enough anywhere on the English coast. On the contrary, although there would be great costs involved, such a scenario has already had potential sites noted.

In 1962 the nuclear arms race was the foremost issue on people's minds. The annual May Day march and rally was due to take place, and as usual a committee drawn from the Glasgow City Labour Party, the Co-operative Party and the Trades Council made the arrangements. It was the City Labour Party's turn that year to choose the main speaker for the rally, and being dominated by leadership loyalists they chose Hugh Gaitskell, the leader of the party, who was very hostile to the CND. He was sure to use this opportunity to further his attack on the peace movement.

In retaliation, the Trades Council, whose turn it was to choose the theme of the march, chose 'No To Polaris'. Trouble was brewing. On the march to Queen's Park, Arnold Wesker, the left-wing playwright, was at the front, CND badge on his lapel, striding along beside Dora Gaitskell, the leader's wife. The march arrived at the bandstand, and a cry was heard, 'Banners up!' Instead of furling the banners as usual, they were displayed to show the variety of trade unions, Labour Party organisations and socialist societies that demanded nuclear disarmament.

As Gaitskell was introduced to the platform, someone in the audience shouted, 'Inspire us!' Wesker thought some toady was going over the top. Janey Buchan had to explain to him, amid the laughter, that this was Glaswegian sarcasm.

Some began to leave their seats before Gaitskell started to speak. They had planned to do so. Instead of responding with a quip, or recognising sincere disagreement while maintaining his own position, he attacked the peace movement, shouting 'You're nothing. You're just peanuts!' Roars of disapproval went up. More and more rose to walk out, seeing no reason why they should sit and hear themselves insulted. Johnny Urquart, the husband of Bunty, a party official, tried to stop them and urge them back in. No chance. 'You can't let the press print pictures of people walking out on the leader's speech', he implored. 'Well, we wouldn't if he was behaving himself,' came the reply. As the argument went on around the entrance gate, the melee grew, and the police piled into the bandstand. I saw no more from my vantage point on the hillside overlooking the bandstand, as I had to go. I had promised to visit my newly married brother Joe and his wife Margaret, away in Woodside on the other side of the city. There was no phone in their flat yet, and I was already very late. I hadn't anticipated all this excitement. I only found out later what a shambles it had all been. A big investigation followed. A Scottish party official turned up unannounced on my parents' doorstep and asked me what I knew of secret plans to disrupt Gaitskell's speech. Nothing was the answer, but he didn't believe me. Like many others, I was threatened with expulsion for being unco-operative. My dad took exception to this arrogant behaviour and wrote a letter of complaint. In the Woodside constituency party, to which most of my friends belonged, the young members got a grilling. There were threats that Woodside would be disbanded. But the Co-operative Party women, who liked the youngsters, stood up for them and shooed the officials away.

The risk of nuclear warfare concerned us in a way that can hardly be imagined today. The Berlin Wall had been built in August 1961. In the event of a nuclear war the Holy Loch would be a prime target. International tension was high. Then in October 1962 our worst fears seemed as if they might be fulfilled: the Cuban missile crisis commenced. Kennedy's and Kruschev's brinkmanship had the world on tenterhooks. No one who lived through that time will ever forget it. As the crisis deepened day by day, and both nuclear superpowers put themselves on full alert, the world waited with bated breath. We were told full alert meant that bombers were already in the air, waiting to be given their orders.

I was at my desk in the gas board's George Square office, in the city centre close to the City Chambers, on the Saturday morning. We thought we might all be dead in a few days' time, and we went to work. No one was actually doing any work. We were glued to the frequent news bulletins on the radios we had brought in. We had been told there would be a four minute warning of a nuclear attack. Later the same day, when in bed at night, I was woken by sirens sending their shrill message and I thought, 'So this is it.' It wasn't, of course. It turned out to be a fire at the mental hospital at Hawkhead, a few miles away. You would think the experience of the world facing the risk of nuclear destruction would have concentrated people's minds, but no. There are now plans to update Trident, kept secret from us by our own government.

When Hugh Gaitskell died, Harold Wilson became leader, and he was much better at uniting the party. Wilson appealed to left-wingers, quoting Aneurin Bevan and his talk of taking over the 'commanding heights of the economy'. His credentials as an economist impressed. He frequently got the better of the Tory front bench with his sharp repartee. It was he who first remarked 'We know what happens to people who stay in the middle of the road. They get run over.' The members responded to adverse media comment, saying 'He might be a tricky bastard, but he's our tricky bastard.' But none of us had a crystal ball, and 1962 was one of the most despair-ridden years I can remember in all my years in politics. We really thought we might not live much longer, even when that crisis had passed.

Then in 1963 there was the John Profumo affair when he, while Conservative Secretary of State for War, had an affair with an alleged call-girl named Christine Keeler, who was chummy with a Soviet army intelligence officer. There were lurid tales of orgies. Profumo was caught out lying to the House of Commons about it. All this led to the collapse of Harold Macmillan's government, and in came Sir Alec Douglas-Home, who confessed on TV that he needed matchsticks to help him follow economic arguments. *That Was the Week that Was*, the satirical late Saturday night TV show, gave him pelters. *Private Eye*, then a new publication, lampooned the Tories. Today we take politicians being satirised for granted. So much so that I, for one, fear we are at risk of endangering democracy if the general public distrusts any and all politicians. Those who have shown they do not deserve trust have deservedly been shown up, but it has all been damaging to the many who are good and honest public servants. But back then, in the early '60s, all this scepticism and poking fun was new. Change was in the air.

Being admirers of Bertrand Russell, of course we had to go a step further than mere membership of CND, and with our friends George Williamson and Walter Morrison, who were the leading lights, we set up a Committee of 100 in Glasgow, to further non-violent peaceful protest. Such groups were springing up all over Britain. We soon realised we had attracted the attention of the plain clothes police. How else do you explain two new members, never seen before at any marches or meetings, with short neat haircuts and shiny boots? One of them offered to take the minutes of the meeting but was politely turned down. 'We'll never see him again', said Jim presciently.

On the 1963 Easter Aldermaston march a leaflet entitled 'Danger: Official Secret' was circulated by the Spies for Peace, a campaigning group who had discovered the whereabouts of the top secret regional seats of government that were already built underground in case a nuclear war should break out. The leaflet pinpointed their locations, and even disclosed their phone numbers. This aroused great interest amongst us, because the government had recently distributed to the general public a leaflet telling them that in the event of nuclear war breaking out they would have a four minute warning to get indoors and shelter under tables. Margie McGowan and I were in one of the teams of volunteers in the gas industry, intended to deal with emergency work and provide first aid when the all-clear was sounded.

When we got back home Jim and I and some of our mates circulated copies of the Spies for Peace leaflet around the Glasgow pubs. We were highly excited about it, and the media were in a furore. It was front page news in every daily. Early arrests were predicted but, although hundreds of people were involved throughout the UK, no one ever was. It has to be admitted that the public read about it, and the public did not rise up in revolt. My dad said, irritatingly, 'Well, wouldn't you expect the government to have the sense to create somewhere safe from which to govern, if there was anything left to govern?'

We felt confident we were not informing the Russians of anything they did not know already. How would peace activists get hold of such information, if Soviet spies couldn't? That didn't stop the Tory press from accusing all concerned of sedition and being in the pay of the enemy. And Defiance of Authority – to which we would plead guilty. Authority, as practised by that Conservative government, won itself no respect.

Two Special Branch policemen interviewed me at home in pursuit of their investigations. As one closed his notebook he said to me, 'You'll end up a Labour MP.' What nonsense, I thought. Hardly any women were MPs.

When Jim and I got engaged, my brother Jim, on one of his rare visits back home from California, went to visit my fiancé's family. He asked Jim's dad what he thought of our sit-downs and generally odd behaviour. My future father-in-law took a puff on his pipe, shook his head, and said, 'As God made them, He matched them.' At our wedding reception on a freezing April day in 1964, the priest made everyone laugh by telling them we were the only couple for whom he had ever officiated who had met each other sitting down in the road, instead of on our feet dancing. At that time Jim was working as a railway clerk and we rented a rundown tenement flat in a city centre street that has long since been demolished. Our address – Parliamentary Road – was the cause of endless quips about our taking the parliamentary road to Socialism. This building had not deteriorated into a slum: it was a slum when it was built. We chose this insalubrious spot because it was within a short walking distance of Strathclyde University, one of the 'new' universities which had grown out of the Royal College of Science and Technology. Jim had been accepted as a mature student to study for a social sciences degree. Soon his wages would stop, and we wanted a cheap rent and to save on bus fares. My mother was utterly horrified that her daughter could even contemplate living in a flat the likes of which she had joyfully escaped decades ago. Can't say I blame her. But we were confident this would last for only a few years until Jim qualified.

The building was poorly maintained by a private sector factor. We found the other tenants did not know they had any legal rights. The electric wiring was so ancient it made an electrician friend laugh in disbelief. Jim and I had come from comfortable, well maintained council-run houses, and had the energy to battle with the factors. We made them install new front doors for everyone and repair the dangerous staircase.

My pride and joy was an ancient mahogany dresser with leaded glass panels in the cupboard doors. I had bid 10s for it at the Crown auction rooms in Sauchiehall Street, or 50 pence in today's money. It cost me £1 to get it delivered, by one of the last remaining horse and cart delivery men. Best bargain I ever had. It was sold at auction some years ago for 200 quid.

We fell about laughing when one visitor, an upper middle class socialist from London, looked around our tiny home with approval and remarked earnestly to us, 'It just shows what the working class can do.' We had two good wages coming in and were better educated than most people living in such conditions. But maybe our neighbours would not have done something as stupid as clever clogs me.

The day we were about to flit to a council flat in Drumchapel I was home alone in the morning, while Jim was out directing a chum who owned a van to our address. I was trying to remove the lampshades from the overhead light fittings and getting nowhere. They were stuck fast. I didn't know that plastic rusts. We could not afford to leave them behind, and besides, why give all these free gifts to our miserly landlord? So, I cut through the flexes with my kitchen scissors, having first, as I thought, taken the necessary precaution by turning off the switches on the walls. I had not turned off the supply at the mains. I was oblivious to the danger of ancient wiring. When Jim came home and spotted the flexes hanging loose from the ceilings, and asked me why, he nearly fainted on the spot. His face paled. 'Will you please leave these jobs to me,' he said, 'before you get yourself killed.' But the comic thing was, Jim was no more expert at DIY than I was. Anything more complicated than a paint brush had us defeated. For years our bookshelves consisted of wooden planks separated by bricks.

Jim and I avoided the Trotskyism bug, but we did join an organisation called Solidarity – nothing to do with either Lech Wałęsa's movement in Poland or Tommy Sheridan's party many years later. Solidarity's magazine poked fun at the convolutions of Trotskyist thought, and generally argued a libertarian socialist and syndicalist line. It had no time for the infighting amongst the sects battling for attention within the Labour youth movement, but preferred action in the workplace where advances could be won if fought for with energy, imagination and determination. They had contacts in Paris too, and in late 1964 some of us travelled there from Glasgow in an old beat-up van to meet like-minded people, the *Socialisme ou Barbarie* group. Later they were to be engaged in the student uprising of 1968.

This was heady stuff. Here we were, in the Latin Quarter, discoursing with people from a foreign country about left-wing politics. Their English was a lot better than our French, which was why we were able to do it at all. Some of us had never even set foot abroad before. In a bistro off the Boulevard Saint-Michel – or the '*Boule Miche*' as we learned to call it casually – one of our number, Ian Mooney, who had almost white blond hair and blue eyes, tried to order '*Cinq bieres, s'il vous plait*' in his guttural Glaswegian accent. My school French was sufficient to let me understand the barmaid saying to her boss, 'That Boche can stand there all night, but I won't serve him.' The war had been over for 19 years. It was ancient history to us, who had been infants or not even born when it started. But the barmaid thought the luckless Ian was a son of one of the Nazis who had jackbooted their way into her country.

As Stuart Christie (who, sadly, died in August this year and was famously involved in a plot to assassinate General Franco) pointed out in his hugely enjoyable memoir *Granny Made Me an Anarchist*, while others were deeply involved in the internecine warfare in the Labour Party, Solidarity organised community action against homelessness and published investigative exposes of conditions within all sorts of industries. They loved poking fun at the inconsistencies and illogicalities of politicians on all parts of the spectrum. They published a song called 'The Workers' Bomb', to the tune of 'The Red Flag', which mocked those who argued Britain should take unilateral steps to divest itself of nuclear weapons, but the Soviet Union should not even diminish its stockpiles, because their bomb was the workers' bomb, so that made it all right. You could take comfort from that thought if they ever – and it would only be in retaliation against an American pre-emptive strike – sent one of their missiles whizzing towards the Polaris base on Holy Loch. I've always liked their style but realised after a while that I simply felt more at home in the Labour Party.

Outside the world of politics, the biggest news was the murders committed by Bible John. This was the sobriquet made up by a newspaper reporter, the police having briefed the media about the descriptions given by the victims' friends of a man who got talking with them in nearby pubs when they went dancing at the Barrowland Ballroom. This man made references to the Bible in his conversation – not the usual chat-up line in those parts, or indeed anywhere. This whole episode seemed to impinge on everyone in Glasgow. Women were afraid to go anywhere alone at night.

By then we were living in a flat in Drumchapel, a huge housing scheme in the north-west of the city, and we had a neighbour downstairs, a mother of three, who regularly went to the Barrowland Ballroom with some of her chums when her husband was on the night shift. The two little ones were left in the charge of her 15-year-old son. One night she was up dancing with a guy who asked if she had ever spoken with any man who talked about the Bible. She confirmed she had, just the previous week, when she was in a pub with some friends. Then her partner revealed he was a policeman and asked her to come down to the station and look through photographs for them. She did so willingly but did not realise she would be hours and hours at her task. And so her husband came home before she did. The reason I know all this is that she ran screaming upstairs to our flat to seek protection from him. Her fears were well grounded. When I refused to let him in he kicked in the door to our flat, but then recovered himself. He realised he had gone much too far. He calmed down and apologised. But it took a while for her to feel safe to return to her own home.

In the mid-'60s it was all the rage to form a commune, sharing a large flat amongst several inhabitants. Jim thought it sounded fun, but I flatly refused. 'The women will end up doing the cooking and cleaning while the men sit around all day discussing politics,' I argued.

Jim laughed. 'Just a wee bourgie girl at heart, aren't you?' he teased. But he, the first one in his family to go to university, was in reality no more willing than I was to throw aside that opportunity.

I was not the only one with a jaundiced view of the division of labour in these set-ups. The women's movement was getting under-way. We were to hear of women who became feminists after partic-ipating in left-wing movements in America, where they had experi-enced exactly what I predicted. The men wrote the pamphlets and the women ran them off on the copying machines. The men knew how to change the world, but not how to operate a Gestetner.

When our first baby, Stephen, was born in 1965, and Chris the following year, further doses of reality kicked in for Jim and me. Asked to contribute to a fighting fund for people facing court action for demonstrating against the fascist colonels who ruled Greece at the time, I very much wanted to, but simply could not. We barely had enough money to get by. I had made two maternity dresses for myself, hand sewn with tiny stitches, for want of a sewing machine.

Jim was a mature student at the time, and we were living on his grant (which was a generous level of funding, by the way, thanks to that 1964 Labour Government, compared to the lot of students today), my occasional earnings from casual secretarial work and his own wages as a postman in the pre-Christmas rush and sum-mertime bus conducting.

We had no spare money for the unforeseen. So it was a quanda-ry one night when Jim had an unforgettable accident. He was play-ing with Stephen and Chris and took one of those educational toys that consist of a rubber sucker held fast to the floor, with a wooden stick inserted, down which the child has to push wooden rings of varying sizes in descending order. Jim thought it much more fun to stick it to the middle of his forehead, pretending to be an animal with a horn on its head. As he turned this way and that, our white sheepskin fireside rug wrapped around him, growling and pounc-ing at the two of them, they were in fits of laughter. It was my turn to laugh when he couldn't get it off.

We tugged and tugged, to no avail. I tried probing at the edges of the sucker pad with soapy water. Useless. Jim urged me to try in-serting a knife, but I was afraid I might dig too hard. So eventually I gave up and said, 'You'll have to go down to the Western and see if they can get it off.' Jim was horrified. 'I can't go there. I'll look really stupid. Imagine everyone on the bus. They'll be killing themselves.'

'Well, you'll just have to take a taxi, then.'

'A taxi! We can't spare the money for a taxi.'

Eventually I persuaded him to give in and call a taxi. The driver could hardly start the motor for laughing. But the casualty department had, no doubt, seen it all before, and swiftly got it off. Jim walked the five miles home. His large, circular red bruise stayed on his forehead for weeks, arousing comment which he declined to answer.

It was a struggle paying the rent, and careful budgeting was needed to ensure our young sons had everything they needed. Jim and I shared one parka between us: when we went out together I got to wear it. I could have written the Oxfam cookbook in those days, always looking for cheap, nourishing food. I had reasoned that, poor as we were by British standards, most of the world lived on incomes much lower than ours, so what did they eat? Lentil curries and rice were incredibly cheap. Eggs featured so hugely in our diet that after he graduated, and was earning a salary, for years Jim never wanted to see an egg, no matter whether it was boiled, poached, fried, or scrambled.So, living such a cash-strapped existence, I thought anyone with a grain of common sense ought to realise that good causes, however good, had to come after feeding and clothing your children. So, very sorry and all that, but the campaign against the Greek colonels would have to get by without me. I resented being thought mean or unsupportive. I admit I did have the mutinous thought that the guys I was being asked to help fund probably spent money in the pub that I couldn't afford. Traditional Labour politics was beckoning once again. It was not about becoming a Labour MP. It was about how best to get things done.

The doom merchants of 1960 had been proved wrong. Harold Wilson projected Labour as a fresh and invigorating force. The contrast with Alec Douglas-Home – the 14th Earl, as Wilson never tired of reminding everyone – could not have been more marked. Labour won a narrow victory in 1964, with a majority of only four seats, and went on to win in 1966 with 13 million votes – 48 per cent of the total. The 13 wasted years were well and truly over. Jim and I wanted to push Labour leftwards.

Chapter 11

'We're no' awa' tae bide awa"

JIM AND I BENEFITED hugely from the creation of New Towns to cope with the scale of need. It was 1970 when we left Drumchapel and moved to Cumbernauld, delighted with the upturn in our living conditions. But our delight was not shared by my mother, thinking she would see me far less often. It was only ten minutes longer on the bus from Glasgow city centre than to our flat in Drumchapel, but she was not to be consoled. Even travelling on a blue Alexander's bus, instead of the familiar orange, cream and green Glasgow Corporation bus just made our move seem all the more foreign.

'It's so far away,' she complained. 'Why can't you stay in Glasgow?'

With not a little exasperation I replied, 'Dear God, you'd think we were going to Australia.'

'No need to take God's holy name in vain,' she replied tearfully. I was adamant that the needs of my children came first. My mother's generation were seemingly more accustomed to putting the wishes of their mothers first. Stephen had just turned five, and the p rimary schools in Glasgow were only offering half-time education up to the age of seven. Cumbernauld, on the other hand, had full time education, and it had pedestrian footpaths away from the traffic. That meant safety to play outdoors, and a safe route home when the boys became old enough not to need picked up from school. Those were days when children walked to school, and few of us had cars anyway.

Now we had a house in a terrace of four dwellings, with our own back garden. I thought the boys would love it at first sight, but when they clapped eyes on it their faces fell. 'What's the matter?' I asked.

Stephen spoke up for both. 'There's no chimney. How will Santa get in?' That was another advantage of our new home – central heating.Two incidents from their early primary years stand out in this proud mother's memory. Stephen, at the age of five, drew an accurate map (which I still have) of the route from his school to our home, putting points of interest in the right place, such as the shop where I bought the papers and bottles of lemonade. Chris was a reason for worry to Mrs Drake, his Primary One teacher, but a cause of hilarity to me. She called me over when I went to collect the boys one day and told me how concerned she was. She had been telling the class about Adam and Eve and the snake talking to them in the Garden of Eden, and Chris, with a very disbelieving ex-pression on his face, had said, 'You just made that up, didn't you?' Neither did he believe Mrs Drake when she told the class that the plaster gnome she had put in a corner of the room could tell her who had been talking when she was out. As he thought this was rubbish he went up to it to prove that it couldn't tell. At this point Mrs Drake walked in and thought Chris had believed her and was talking to the gnome. He wasn't best pleased.

When my dad died in 1972 my mother came to stay with us for a few years before being allocated a flat of her own nearby. I had been very fond of my dad and had fully expected to look after him in his old age, anticipating my mum would die first, as she was the one with the poor health over so many years, whereas he had been fit and well until the very recent past. Mum felt unable to live alone in what had been the family home in Pollok. Jim invited her to stay with us, which meant a change of family doctor, and for the first time in years she was seen by a GP who cared about getting her dose of tranquilliser right – it had been far too high – and he also told her she was diabetic. Mum's diet sheet advised that she should avoid alcoholic drinks, except for a small amount of very dry sher-ry. As she had never been a drinker, this was not a problem. But she read this advice to mean she should drink some sherry and asked me to get her a bottle. And so it came to pass that one day, when she was minding the kids on their return from school until I got back from university, I came home to find her feeling very ill and wondering what was wrong with herself.

'Oh Maria, thank goodness you're back. I feel terrible. My head hurts, but it's not like my normal headaches. I feel weak and unsteady. And I feel as if I'm going to pass out.'

Then I noticed the sherry bottle on the table. It was nearly half empty. A few black coffees later, and plenty of water to drink, eventually convinced her she wasn't at death's door.

'Why do people drink this stuff,' she plaintively asked, 'if it makes them feel like that?'

When Mum moved into a nearby flat of her own, it was because our GP had advised me that Stephen, who was asthmatic, ought to have a bedroom of his own and avoid sharing a bunk bed with his brother. So that meant she would have to go, but at least it was only a short distance away. And that meant I had to drop in on her every day to ensure she had taken all her tablets. She was far from happy with this arrangement, telling me I ought to put her needs first, but I disagreed. It's not as if she had been happy in my house either, never feeling able to settle. In truth, Jim's mother was a generous and kindly granny, always keen to see her grandchildren. My mother refused to have the children call her 'Gran' or any other diminutive of 'grandmother' because it made her feel old. She said 'Mrs O'Neill' was the appropriate form of address. I think she badly missed Dad, the only one who always put her first, and she had little or no capacity to adjust to widowhood.

We were now tenants of Cumbernauld Development Corporation, whose views of tenants' rights were as limited as any local authority of the time. People would come home from work to find huge pictures painted on their gable end. No one had thought to inform, never mind ask the tenants their views on having a 30-foot golden eagle decorating the side wall of their home.

One day we came home to find our front door painted khaki. Well, that was the polite description of the colour. When we complained we were told that tenants could not choose their own colour as their taste might not be acceptable to either the Corporation or the neighbours. Which might, in some cases, be true enough. But had they found a majority who would choose khaki above all other colours? No, of course not.

Jim believed in direct action when conventional approaches proved useless. He bought a pot of paint in the dreariest shade of
mud brown he could find, went straight to the front door of the
chairman of the development corporation, and began to give it a
clean prior to painting it. Nothing if not thorough. The pot of paint
sat open on the doorstep, with his brush across the top. He was
soon accosted by someone in the household.

'What do you think you're doing?' he cried. Jim lifted the brush, dipped it in the paint, and raised it to the door, whistling
'McAlpine's Fusiliers' as he did so.

'Same as got done to my door,' he answered.

'Do you think you have a right to come here and do this?'

'The Development Corporation thinks it's OK to do this to my
door.'

'Wait a minute. Wait a minute. No need for this. I'll make sure
this is looked into.'

A few days later an official came round our neighbourhood saying we could have any colour we wanted from the palette of four
or five he had to show.

The anarchic streak in Jim's character was never far below the
surface. Once, when we were on a huge anti-unemployment march
through Glasgow city centre, we noticed that the band that accompanied a National Union of Miners' (NUM) branch in Ayrshire was
obviously from an Orange Lodge. There were numerous flute players who had the characteristic swaying walk, and the huge drum
being battered with a will had written around it something about
being 'Loyal Sons of William'.

It horrified some members of our Labour Party branch that such
a sectarian outfit was on a Labour movement demonstration. Jim
and I took the opposite view. We argued that the important thing
was to gather as much support as possible against the scourge of
unemployment. If that meant drawing in people who would not
normally march with us, then that was all to the good. They might
learn some progressive politics while they were about it.

Others in the branch were not convinced. They moved that a

letter be sent to the NUM branch concerned, urging them to avoid sectarian bands in future. Jim moved as an amendment that the message should be delivered, not by post, but in person, by the mover and seconder of the motion. They should visit these burly Ayrshire miners and tell them where they had got it wrong. The mover laughed disbelievingly. 'Was Jim serious?'

'Absolutely,' he answered. 'Shouldn't we have the courage of our convictions?' Jim's amendment won a majority, the members tee-heeing as they voted for it, but I don't think the message ever got delivered as directed. There were always too many other things for busy people to be doing.

I was less anarchic than Jim. If truth be told, I can be so determined that decisions taken will be do-able and be carried out, on time and within budget, that I have been nicknamed 'Stalin's Auntie'. One night a *Militant* 'reader' made the mistake of visiting our house to try to sell us a copy. Jim signalled a message to me with his eyes, clearly saying 'Let's have some fun with this one.' He argued an anarchist line with him, asking why the working class should pay any attention to this guy's guru, Ted Grant, or any other self-appointed leader. I threw in everything I had ever heard on the subject of why Stalin had it in for Trotsky. Keeping my face straight, I expressed the view that, if anything, Stalin was too soft. As he headed out the door, confused and upset, he said, 'And you two are married to each other?'

When he graduated in Social Sciences at Strathclyde University Jim wanted to enter journalism. He came home one day bouncing with delight, as he had got a job with the *Sunday Post*. This paper, an institution in Scottish life, has been known to generations of Scottish families for its Oor Wullie and The Broons cartoons, and regular features such as Francis Gay's Diary telling heart-warming stories, the Hon Man awarding cash to anyone carrying a copy of the *Post* who recognised him as he strolled around one of our seaside towns, and 'The Doc'.

The reporters also took their turn at writing the medical advice column. Jim at least had enough sense of responsibility to check his 'copy' with a friend who was a GP before submitting it. This was not always the case with some of his colleagues, who looked up ailments in medical dictionaries instead. One time the picture editor wanted a photo of a virus that was in the news, as it was causing widespread experience of unpleasant symptoms, and disappointedly turned it down when Jim brought back from a laboratory a picture of a small collection of cells. He had thought the virus, blown up to many times its size, would look like some scary creature with bug eyes, hairy legs and sharp teeth.

But such was the trust placed in the *Post* by its readers that Boots protested to them that if they were going to recommend some over-the-counter medication, would they please forewarn them as they were constantly running out of stock in response to the demand.

The DC Thomson empire were very anti-trade union. Jim regarded it as a matter of principle to join the National Union of Journalists (NUJ) and start secretly recruiting. About a year or so later he joined the *Sunday Mail*, and his successor at his old post was sacked when the management found out about his recruiting members for the NUJ.

When the student revolt broke out in Paris in 1968 Jim wrote a double page spread for the *Sunday Mail*, giving the impression he was right there on the boulevards witnessing it all. He wasn't. He simply phoned the people we had met a few years before, when we had been on our visit to Paris to meet fellow socialists and was put in touch with good contacts amongst the student leadership.

Jim had got through university; now it was my turn. I chose Strathclyde on the grounds that it was nearer home than Glasgow University, so it would be easier to fit classes in with childcare. I picked Economic History as one of the five subjects every first year arts and social sciences student had to take, because its timetable fitted better than other subjects with my need to get home before school was out. I had been no great student of History at school, and everyone told me there was so much information to take in it was a downright stupid thing to do. All the other students would have a Higher or an A Level and be so much better prepared. Yet it turned out to be one of the best decisions I have ever made. I loved it. I found every aspect of it fascinating. I could happily study for hours when the subject interested me, and I ended up choosing it when I went on to do an Honours.

Studying Economic History without great attention to the Industrial Revolution and subsequent developments is like Rock 'n' Roll without Elvis Presley. And that is my excuse for one of the silliest decisions I have ever made. I was mentally time travelling back to the age of the Reform Act and the Chartists' fight for democratic reforms. I was paying scant attention to the world I was actually living in.Have you ever felt embarrassed by your own stupidity? If I am ever asked that question I know how I would reply. Yes. It is when I look back on my decision to join Jim Sillars in the Scottish Labour Party (SLP). It started out looking good. To the left of the Labour Party? Tick. Caring about the Scottish dimension? Tick. Democratic rights for members? Tick.

I went along to the founding meeting in January 1976 at the Grosvenor Hotel in Glasgow. The room was packed with around 400 people. My husband Jim had joined the 'mini-cadre' of hardline devolutionists that conceived the new party, and for a short time he was a member of its national organising committee. Not normally impressed by oratory, I sat there cheering inwardly at Jim Sillars' rousing, passionate speech. He demanded 'a strong Scottish Parliament working within the broad framework of the United Kingdom'. As a member of the executive of the Labour Party's Scottish Council, and the holder of the largest Labour majority in Scotland (where thumping majorities had been commonplace) he had a lot of credibility. So why did it all go wrong?

There were reasons that seemed compelling at the time for its creation. At that time the Labour Party was split. Some wanted devolved powers for Scotland, believing it would foster more socialist policies that way than could be hoped for from the benighted souls down south. Others were utterly opposed, fearing it would break up the United Kingdom, and seeing this as counter to our party's internationalism. No one in the Labour Party wanted Scotland to break away from the rest of Britain, but some of us had begun to think that our people would be better served by a sister party operating in Scotland, just as the Social Democratic and Labour Party did in Northern Ireland. Recent history did nothing to reassure us that anything less than a copy of the SDLP was going to resolve the problem.

Winnie Ewing had won Hamilton in a by-election, overturning a huge Labour majority, and became the sole SNP MP. When it came to the municipal elections in 1968, the SNP made a net gain of 103 seats.

In 1968 the Labour Party Scottish Conference rejected devolution by a large majority. Then in March 1969 the Executive of the Scottish Council of the Labour Party put its opposition to devolution on record. The following month Harold Wilson set up a Royal Commission, later to produce the Kilbrandon Report, advocating devolution. It worked to Labour's advantage in Scotland, delivering a majority of seats in the 1970 General Election. However, the Conservatives won an unexpected victory overall, and that meant devolution was kicked into the long grass for quite a while.

Then in 1973 Labour's Scottish Council reaffirmed its opposition to devolution in a pamphlet. Within a few weeks the SNP gained Glasgow Govan in a by-election, their candidate was the young Margo MacDonald. An intelligent and lively woman, the media chose to dub her 'the blonde bombshell', as if her hair was the most interesting thing to say about her.In the General Election that followed in February 1974, during a nationwide miners' strike, Harold Wilson formed a minority government. Ted Heath had called the election, asking, 'Who governs Britain? The government or the miners?' and the electorate had answered, 'Not you, at any rate.' The SNP won six new seats, two gained from Labour, and won 22 per cent of votes cast in Scotland. A poll privately commissioned by Labour showed another 13 seats could be lost to the SNP at the next election – and that could be any time soon. Wilson therefore promised a devolution White Paper in the Queen's Speech that opened the new Parliament.

In June the Scottish Executive of the party met at short notice to discuss the issue. Scotland had reached the final stages of the World Cup and was playing Yugoslavia in Frankfurt that day, and 18 of the committee members absented themselves. Those who turned up rejected all devolution schemes offered by the Labour Government by six votes to five. The Labour Party's national executive was appalled. Further losses to the SNP could only be expected if this anti-devolution policy remained in force. The SNP, after decades in the wilderness, had been gaining ground. What were voters in Scotland to make of such an important decision made by a one vote majority, at a meeting where so many had so little sense of responsibility they had absented themselves to watch football instead of discussing what was best for the future of our people? The National Executive Committee (NEC) called Jimmy Allison, the legendary Labour organiser in Scotland, to London, and told him to ensure the party in Scotland held a conference to reverse the vote.

The famed special conference in the Dalintober Street Co-op Halls that has gone down in Labour history was held that August, two days before the General Election date was announced. It was to be in October. This time the devolution supporters succeeded, with the aid of the trade unions' block vote. It has been alleged that it was not so much that they cared about devolution, but they saw their chance to gain a quid pro quo, and a substantial one at that, affecting the whole of the UK: a social contract on wages. But I had heard passionate speeches supporting devolution at conferences over the years, and this is proved by an examination of the trade unions' own records. It was true, however, that some of the trade unions' leaderships were not all that interested in devolution, and supported motions in its favour simply because they were anxious not to do anything to upset the Labour Government's chances of re-election, and who could blame them for that? But Sillars noted their less-than-enthusiastic support, and it has been said that made him determined not to have block votes when he founded the Scottish Labour Party. When it came to that election campaign, which Labour won with a majority of only four, my husband Jim wrote some of the material in the *Labour News*. This was the first time Labour issued a Scottish manifesto, and it promised to create an Assembly. The SNP reached its highest point until then at Westminster, with 11 seats and just over 30 per cent of the vote.

Then in November 1975 Labour published its White Paper on

a Scottish Assembly, 'Our Changing Democracy'. Crucially, it did not promise 'economic teeth' – in the words of Jim Fyfe who invented that expression for use in party publications. There was no promise in the White Paper to let the Assembly have control over the Scottish Development Association. That was a huge disappointment to all those who wanted a powerful Assembly, with authority to change things for the better. After that, a number of the 'devo max' people began to believe a new Scottish socialist party would have to be formed. And so, inexorably, events led to the formation of the SLP the following January.

Was the newly-formed SLP more socialist than the Labour Party? Judge for yourself. We in the Cumbernauld branch, which I chaired, gave financial and vocal support to the local dustmen, who were on strike. Not for higher pay, but to defend themselves from a cut in pay imposed by the ruling SNP administration. If Sillars had backed us it would have shamed the local Labour Party, who were keeping out of it, and shown up the dishonesty of the SNP's claims to be the alternative party for left-leaning voters.

It has been surmised that Sillars was such a parliamentarian that he could not support any other kind of campaigning, whether it be for striking dustmen or student teachers who had just been told there were no jobs available after three or four years' study. If so, that would not be surprising. There are plenty of politicians who feel uncomfortable with any action outside speeches and votes in Parliament.

As for party democracy, my husband Jim had been experiencing frequent problems with Sillars on the SLP's National Organising Committee (NOC). Sillars, he said, simply was unable to hear any other point of view. The party was his ball, and if others didn't play his way he was taking it home. John Nairn, another member of the NOC, told us that when he put forward an argument he only got a violent stream of abuse in reply.I have to admit I missed a crucial defect in the SLP. The new party would have no trade unions affiliated. Why would they throw away their influence on a governing party, and join a new and untried one that gave them no rights at all?

By creating an ideological party, the SLP attracted teachers, journalists, students, social workers and academics. It lacked skilled and
unskilled workers. Henry Drucker, author of *Breakaway*, an account
of the SLP's early days, pointed out, 'these members were writers of
pamphlets, signers of petitions, framers of resolutions, not party loyalists.' There was widespread antipathy to authority in many SLP
activists, and the SLP turned out to be something that did not meet
their aims.

By its first Congress in October 1976 everything had collapsed.
The party had been infiltrated by a small number of Trotskyists
from the IMG, who had judged they could spend their members'
time more profitably within the SLP than in the Labour Party. But
there were never more than 15 IMG members in the SLP at any one
time.

Sillars was determined to root them out. Considering there were
never more than 30 IMG members in the whole of Scotland, it is
hard to see how they could have been an overwhelming influence
on a party claiming some 2,000 members. It was partly Sillars' fear
of media criticism, and partly his unwillingness to countenance any
source of opposition, that made him take the IMG far too seriously.
But it was his way of dealing with disagreement that I could not
stand.

Disloyalty was suspected if anyone dared to disagree. But it was
becoming clear there was division of opinion over membership of
the European Community, and there was an as yet unresolved debate over 'devo max' and on whether separation from the rest of
the UK should be supported. Some of us were strongly opposed.
That was not what we joined the SLP for. Still, we wanted a proper
debate to resolve the matter.

The Cumbernauld branch wrote to the NOC, protesting against
Congress not being given its place to make policy decisions. We
were fed up with the leadership making personal statements that
were presented as policy.

At the October Congress in the Red Lion Hotel in Stirling, I
was horrified on the Friday night to learn that a decision had been
made to suspend the entire Leith branch and seven named alleged

members of the IMG. No charges were substantiated. None were given a chance to state their case. Calls for evidence were shouted down. I went to the rostrum to argue this was unjust. By all means, I argued, expel anyone who was proved to have been acting in any way harmful to the party. But what kind of justice was it, I argued, that found someone guilty with no opportunity to state their defence? Otherwise we were just running a kangaroo court, and I would never support that.

Then the NOC decided to disband a further four branches: Kelvin, Stirling, Stirling University and Cumbernauld – the branches that had been expressing disagreement on policy issues and objecting to the way the leadership made no attempt to seek the views of the membership.

An emergency resolution to that effect was read out on the Sunday morning. Wild applause roared. Baying voices shouted, 'Get them out... out... out.' There was no discussion, calls for evidence were shouted down. When I tried to go to the rostrum to defend my branch and seek a debate I was roughly pushed aside by a party official and fell to the floor. New stewards – not those elected by Congress – had a highly aggressive demeanour. We did not know of what we were accused, but clearly to defend human rights was to be suspect oneself. A large number of delegates were opposed to these suspensions, at least until they had heard any evidence, but John Robertson (the sole other MP who had joined, and not the one who later became MP for Garscadden) and Jim Sillars threatened to resign if the suspensions were not approved. Sillars defended this action with words that can still chill me: 'At times of crisis, working class organisations expel without discussion.' He uttered another phrase to support his actions: 'Mak siccar'. Normally anyone might simply say, 'Make sure', but these words were chosen to convey something weightier and steelier, recalling battles fought long ago. I had a vague feeling that this phrase had some kind of origin in Scottish history, and sure enough I learned that when Robert the Bruce stabbed Comyn (a rival for the throne of Scotland) in the monastery in Dumfries, and came out saying 'I think I have killed Comyn', one Roger Kirkpatrick said 'I mak siccar' and went in and stabbed Comyn in the heart. Well, we do make advances in civilisation. Sillars only meant expulsion.

Considering that of all the 32 people expelled at Sillars' behest at the Stirling Congress only one was an active IMG member, and further considering no one was contemplating battling with Sillars to the death, this choice of language seems a trifle OTT. But then it is noticeable in some Scottish politicians that when they want to sound forceful they go verrry Scottish, as if plain English could not do the job sufficiently well.

The Cumbernauld members' heads rolled that day too. I went home in tears, full of rage and disappointment that it had come to this. The entire sorry affair was only rubbed in all the more sorely when I turned on the radio and heard Donald Dewar, who had a job at that time commenting on political affairs for Radio Clyde, enjoying the whole debacle. Only through the media did we finally find out that we were accused of being infiltrators from the IMG or, more broadly, 'left-wing extremists'. It has to be said that many journalists held views in common with Sillars, and not many in the media informed the public that the IMG influence was wildly exaggerated. Little or no attempt was made to contact any expelled members for their side of the story. It was left to Jim Mackechnie, who later became a Labour councillor, to sum up in a letter to *The Scotsman*:

> A party which expels rather than debates becomes a party of sycophants, careerists and unprincipled opportunists. It loses all credibility, dynamism and respect. Henry Drucker [author of *Breakaway*] has done a service to Scottish politics by cataloguing the various stages of putrefaction of the SLP. All that now remains to be effected is the burial of the corpse.

Our branch was not going to let Sillars have the cash resources we had built up. We wound the branch up the following month, gave a large donation to the dustmens' strike fund, and used the remainder to throw a party that lasted three days.

Chapter 12

'Take Me Home'

MEANWHILE JIM AND I had more bother to contend with. Jim had been promoted to chief industrial reporter for *The Glasgow Herald*. But then the owners of the *Daily Express* and *Glasgow Evening Citizen* closed down the editorial offices and print works in Albion Street creating hundreds of redundancies. Rather than knuckle under, some of the workforce decided to form a co-op and create a new paper, the *Scottish Daily News*, and it was launched in May 1975. Tony Benn, then Secretary of State for Industry in the Labour Government, supported the plan. The new paper was looking for staff, and Jim and I felt he had to join in. All our political lives we had believed in workers' self-management, and now it was put up or shut up. But from day one the paper did not succeed. It failed to achieve the advertising revenue it needed, and that was the co-op's own fault. It was not clear who its target audience were, and that made advertisers think they were better off spending their money elsewhere. It was afraid to offend. Jim had a good story about a bookmaker's firm, that would have made the front page on the *Herald*, but they didn't run it for fear of upsetting some of their advertisers. Such was the dire state of affairs they even looked to Robert Maxwell as a saviour, who already had a poor reputation. Indeed, the co-op learned of a damning report by the Department of Trade and Industry, saying 'Robert Maxwell is not in our opinion a person who can be relied on to exercise proper stewardship of a public company.' Maxwell turned out to be another one that would take his ball away if people didn't play his way. Jim saw the way things were going and went back to the *Herald*.

Having spent a year out of politics following the SLP debacle we applied to re-join the Labour Party. We realised what a big mistake we had made. It was the stupidest thing I have ever done politically. Norman Buchan and Neil Carmichael had been urging us to come back. I knew Norman thought well of me. When Norman was fighting the 1972 election, he asked me to help with a logistical problem in his constituency. With its large rural area West Renfrewshire had numerous villages, many wanting to hear the Labour candidate at a local meeting, and he had to make short visits to two or three on any one night. He wanted me to do the 'warm up' with a supporting speech at one of the meetings, while they waited for his arrival. I had never done that before. I found I could think of additional material to speak about while I was on my feet and keep going... and going... and going while Norman still did not arrive. In desperation I brought out a round sponge cake from my shopping bag and cut it with a borrowed penknife, to illustrate the unfair division of wealth in society. At that time the 7:84 theatre company was putting that message across by its very name: pointing out that a mere 7 per cent of the population held 84 per cent of the country's wealth. Norman arrived to see us all munching away happily and got his breath back while we finished eating.

I wished Jim and I had listened to him when he was advising us not to follow Sillars into the SLP. We had thought Norman's hostility to devolution was the cause, and we did not heed his warnings that we would be unlikely ever to be able to work with a politician like Sillars.

I was struck, for the first time in my life, by the sheer decency of the Labour Party compared to what I had experienced in one short year with the SLP. It had democratic processes. It was conscientious in its efforts to allow anyone accused to be heard. If I was accepted back in I was determined to work for it as never before. This was to lead to unexpected consequences. I still had not the smallest ambition to become a Labour MP, despite encouragement from Norman. After all, look how seldom women became MPs. There was only one Labour woman MP at that time in Scotland, Judith Hart, and before her there had been a grand total of eight since the party was formed at the start of the century. I remembered all too well what happened when a vacancy arose for the General Election in February 1974. The local party members were unanimous in wanting Janey Buchan to be the Labour candidate because she was a well-known councillor, campaigner on consumer issues and supporter of good causes. She was ideal for a constituency like Dunbartonshire East (which included Cumbernauld), where we would be competing with both the SNP and the Conservatives.

But under Labour different rules applied then, people who were not members of our Party could have an equal vote if they belonged to an affiliated organisation, with no need to register support. The Transport and General Workers' Union had a senior steward at Triumph in Cowley, Eddie McGarry, whom they wanted to punt into a Parliamentary seat. The guy had no connection with our area. Came the night of the selection conference and the Union filled busloads of delegates from surrounding garages and outvoted all the rest of us. Then they all disappeared, never to be seen again. When local activists called on some of these T&G delegates at their homes, to ask them to do some election campaigning, they were met at the door by individuals stating they had never even voted Labour. Those who had wanted Janey for our candidate were left to do the door knocking and leaflet delivering to try to get McGarry elected. Several left the party in disgust. Jim and I, and plenty of others, being disciplined comrades, did the leafleting and canvassing, but also complained to party headquarters and got a supportive response.

Our candidate did not manage to win the seat, against a national trend that year that supported the election of a Labour Government. He just did not make the right impression, or indeed much of an impression. It was the Conservative candidate, Barry Henderson, who won the seat. In that election there was an 85 per cent turnout nationally, and at the village hall in Condorrat which was the polling station where I stood giving out leaflets in the snow, I saw an elderly man arrive on a stretcher, determined to vote Labour to keep Edward Heath out of power.

Many years later it was the Transport and General Workers' Union's willingness to nominate me, seek support for me from other unions, and sponsor me, that put me on the shortlist for the constituency of Glasgow Maryhill.

When I qualified as a teacher in 1976, after a year's teacher training at Jordanhill, I applied for a job at Falkirk College of Technology as a General Studies lecturer. At my interview Dr Easton, the Principal, asked me if I was a practical, hands on kind of person. I think he was worried about arts and social sciences people being, as he saw it, airy-fairy, if not downright dotty, unlike the lecturers in the industrial crafts taught there. I showed him my hands, still bearing a greenish hue from the paint I had been applying to an old chest of drawers that very morning.

Then he mentioned that the lads in these classes might be difficult to handle, as they would see me as a woman that couldn't do the skills they were being taught. I replied that, as a Labour Party member, I was constantly at meetings with men who could be their dads, and we got along fine. That seemed to satisfy him. I later realised why he sought these reassurances about my common sense and ability to cope. As soon as I joined the staff I was regaled with the tale of Mr Ian Bowman, the head of the General Studies department, who had some years ago tried out an experiment with one of his classes to show them how people could witness the same incident but truthfully give contradictory accounts of it. His students that day had no forewarning that anything exceptional was going to occur. He had arranged for a student to burst into his classroom, angrily shouting and threatening him, and waving a grenade around. It was an entirely safe keepsake from his days in the armed forces, but his class did not know that. What happened next has gone down in the history of the college. One student threw open the first floor window and jumped out. Another bravely wrestled the supposed assailant to the floor, grabbed the grenade and threw it out the window. Others just sat and gaped. The whole affair was written up by Mr Bowman in an academic journal. If I had been the teacher who enacted this experiment I would have kept very quiet.

I had a class of moulders, seen by the other crafts as the bottom rung of all the trades, who were very pleasant boys and actually called me 'Mum' occasionally. They always did promptly as they were asked.

Another new class was memorable for a quite different reason. This class met in a prefab isolated from the main building. I was compiling their register when I heard a softly spoken chant being repeated by six of the boys seated together in the middle of the room. 'There's going to be a gang bang, there's going to be a gang bang...' it went. I looked up, took in which ones were chanting, and went back to the register. 'Miss, are you not afraid?' a voice came.

'Yeah, terrified' I replied glancing up and turning my attention back to the register. Then, looking sternly at the culprits, I said 'Any more of that and you will be off the course and out of a job.' One boy recklessly asked, 'But you can't do that, can you?'

'No', I replied, 'but Dr Easton, the Principal, certainly would.'

'Sorry miss, oh sorry'.

After that there was no more trouble. But I was amused to over-hear as they left when the bell rang, one boy saying to another, 'She's from Glasgow. They're a tough lot there.'

That'll do me nicely, I smiled to myself.

One very wet morning a student in another class arrived soaked to the skin, having stood a long time waiting for his bus. I said to him, 'You should go home, have a warm bath, change into dry clothes, and just get back as soon as you can. You can't spend all day here in that state. I'll tell your next lecturer I gave you leave.' Whereupon, to my amazement, he started wiping away a tear. 'What's the matter?' I asked.

'That's the first nice thing anyone has said to me since I came here', he replied.

There were some Arab students working in the nearby oil refinery who objected to being taught by a woman. Dr Easton, who was no feminist, told them they would have the staff he had allocated to them or leave the course. They gave in and found they could live with a woman telling them what to do after all.

The Arabs went to the local disco on Saturday nights. One

Monday morning, as the young women in the first year electricians' class were chatting outside the classroom waiting to be let in, I heard them complain that the Arab students had been refused entry by the bouncer. 'It's not fair,' they all stormed.

At last, I thought. My anti-racism message is getting through.

'So why', I asked, 'do you think it's not fair?'

'Because they're rerr dancers, Miss,' they replied.

Apparently the management's decision was based on local young men's complaint that they could not compete with the glamorous Arabs and their sports cars.

In the year of Scotland in the World Cup one young plumber told me he was going to join Ally's Army and go to Argentina on his motorbike. When I asked him how he would cross the ocean, he asked 'Ocean? What ocean?' I am still wondering how anyone can spend four years in secondary school and still not be aware of such basic information about our planet. But then he probably wonders how some customers can do such stupid things with their plumbing.

During this time, I became the Educational Institute of Scotland (EIS) rep for my college. The staff in the General Studies department spent most of their time teaching the craft students, but also taught Highers classes. Then someone in the education authority had decided that, to save money, we should no longer be allowed to teach any subjects at Highers level. We had the relevant degrees, and wanted to keep our hands in. Besides, and this was what really mattered, the college had been giving a second chance to people who, for whatever reason, had not succeeded in academic subjects in their schooldays. We had a pretty good record of results for these students, and this would now be lost. Some of my colleagues made contemptuous remarks about the lack of qualifications held by the councillors on the education committee of the Council. That was never going to help. As EIS rep I composed a letter to Michael Kelly, the education convener, pointing out what a loss this would be to people's hopes. To his credit Michael Kelly overturned the policy soon afterwards and we continued to provide that service.

I enjoyed my days at Falkirk Tech, but a few years later I began a job that I loved. The Trades Union Congress (TUC) were look-ing for local further education colleges to set up units for social sciences graduates to run training courses for union reps, and one such was to be set up at Central College of Commerce in Glasgow. There would be basic courses for new shop stewards and safety reps, and more advanced courses in such matters as bargaining, work study and pensions. I applied, thinking most hopefuls would have a history of experience in the shipyards or other heavy indus-tries. I could not offer such a muscular CV, but I made a virtue of having been an active trade unionist when I worked in the Scottish Gas Board offices, and indeed currently the EIS rep at my college. I was surprised and pleased to discover during my interview that the head of this new unit was to be Jim Whyte, who had been a fellow student at Jordanhill College where we had our teacher training year. Jim had been an active trade unionist when working as a joiner in the shipyards, and like me had gone to university as a ma-ture student. He recommended making me one of his team on the grounds of my kind of experience, but also because we had fought together against the Trots.

I began work as the sole female in our unit. We were a mixed bag politically. Jim and Calum Campbell were Communists, Ben-ny McGowan and I were in the Labour Party, Geoff McCracken moved around politically, and Vladimir Maximiew was a Maoist.

We worked flat out to keep up with the huge demand from lo-cal trade unions. I taught a class of garment workers, whose main problem was the bonus scheme devised by their employer, but which was never explained. What they had worked out was that the more hours they worked, the less per hour they got paid. All the men they knew, in other industries, seemed to get at least the same hourly rate for overtime. Even double and treble time. I worked through the figures with them, they grew in confidence, and with greater strength in numbers negotiated a better deal. But what was additionally gratifying was one of the women telling me that she had never been able to help her son do his arithmetic homework, but now she could, having mastered percentages and other cal-culations she could never do when she was at school. Preparing to tackle the boss had given her the motivation to learn, and her confidence grew with it.

A trained safety rep can do a lot to prevent practices that are unsafe, unhealthy and even lethal. Never having had any experience of heavy industry, I for my part was learning about the risks that manual workers lived with in their daily lives. Men who worked with asbestos had been lied to by their bosses about 'safe levels', of which there is no such thing. Some worked with chemicals that had been banned. Some of the men were too macho to wear safety helmets, and I had to persuade them that their wives and girlfriends would not admire them for it, but only think they were daft.

In this job I got to know hundreds of men and women who were active in their unions, far more than I would otherwise have normally come across. This was significant where my future path was concerned. When the Glasgow Maryhill Constituency Labour Party, of which I was a member, was looking for a candidate in 1985 for the next General Election, I had the support of the T&G, GMB and National Union of Public Employees (NUPE) who knew me from my work.

When the boys reached secondary school age in the late '70s we moved back to Glasgow. Both Jim's job and mine were there, and as the boys got older they would want what the city offered, including not having to get the last bus home at 10.00pm.

We joined Kelvingrove Labour Party, where we already had some friends. The boys getting older meant I had more time to work for the party, in my own mind almost in penance for my earlier aberration. (Once a Catholic, always a Catholic?) I felt more in tune with the values of the Labour Party in a way I had not before. The Tories, under Thatcher, were hell bent on harsh, right-wing policies, making the rich richer and the poor poorer, and had to be opposed.

The Council at that time was 'hung', that is, no party had an overall majority. For the first time in umpteen years Labour had lost its majority and was running a minority administration, brought about by two councillors who had disgracefully misused their positions. One had cheated for her daughter in the housing queue, the other was jailed for fraudulent claims on his council expenses. Then David Hodge, a Labour councillor, became Lord Provost and entertained the South African ambassador. In response to this, Janey Buchan had the idea of making Glasgow the first in the world to offer Nelson Mandela the Freedom of the City, and the City Labour Party enthusiastically supported the idea when moved by Ian Davidson.

The SNP held the balance of power and could not agree amongst themselves what they wanted and then stick to it. Officers could not do any long term planning when there were constant changes of mind over policy. Jean McFadden, leader of the Labour Group, appealed to members to come forward and stand as council candidates. She wanted to put candidates in place in plenty of time for campaigning before the council elections that were due to take place in 1980. I put my hand up. I was selected for Blairdardie Ward, which happened to be the same ward Jim and I had lived in when we had our flat in Drumchapel, so I already knew it well.

On that night I was asked a question that was obviously important to the member, as he had kept holding his hand up waiting for the Chair to call him. He wanted to know, 'Do you think the Soviet Union is a workers' state, a deformed workers' state, or state capitalist?' Memories of those arcane debates in my Young Socialist days came flooding back. But this guy was no Young Socialist, he was older than I was. I hoped I was not losing his vote when I replied that I felt sticking labels on a vast, complex economic and social system, whose good points and bad points we could spend all night discussing, did not really have much point. Tongue in cheek I added that there would be little call for such analysis at meetings of the Housing, Planning, or Parks and Recreation Committees. Although it might be useful to know how local soviets ran such services, and indeed other international comparators might have interesting ideas. He smiled and nodded. He told me later he was just wanting to test whether I was one of those lefties whose brains ran on tramlines.

The SNP had, at the previous district council elections, won all six seats in Garscadden, in the north-west of the city, where Donald Dewar was to begin the renewal of Labour fortunes in Glasgow with his winning the Parliamentary seat in the by-election of 1978, where, incidentally, Jim Sillars' party won only 583 votes. Outside where the votes were being counted, Nationalists flung beer cans and spat on Labour activists.

The SNP did particularly badly in the 1979 General Election, which they brought on themselves by tabling a motion of No Confidence in Jim Callaghan's Labour Government. They were fed up because the government declared in December 1976 that its proposals for a Scottish Assembly would be subject to a referendum. Yet it would hardly be democratic to create such a substantial change in the governance of a country without seeking its electorate's support. The creation of elected Assemblies in Wales and in Scotland was not only a major item in the government's legislative programme. It had been a commitment in the 1974 Manifesto and was approved as party policy by conference.So it was particularly galling that George Cunningham, a Scot who was a Labour MP for a seat in London, and opposed to devolution, put down an amendment on 15 January 1979 to say that 40 per cent of the whole electorate, not simply a majority of those voting, would have to support the creation of the Assembly. It was carried by a majority of 15, although the government was opposed to it, by an alliance of Tories and 34 Labour anti-devolutionists.

The referendum was held on 1 March 1979. Jim and I joined in the campaign, Jim writing material for Labour's Yes campaign. It snowed. It was freezing as we trudged around delivering leaflets. There were strikes in schools, hospitals and public services. Who knows how far all that affected turnout and how people voted. It was the closest of shaves: 1,230,000 voted for, 1,150,000 million against, on a 63.8 per cent turnout.

The referendum resulted in a 51.6 per cent majority in favour, but the yes vote only made 32.9 per cent of the overall electorate, far below the 40 per cent required by the Cunningham amendment. None of the Scottish regions cleared the hurdle, and indeed several had a majority voting against. In spite of such figures, the

Nationalists pressed the government to go ahead with devolution and were angry at not getting their way. Yet, as Andrew Marr has commented:

> It is hard to feel a sense of outrage that an Assembly was not established because less than one third of the electorate wanted it. The argument that big constitutional change should have widespread popular support is hardly an undemocratic one.

From this, as Callaghan wrote,

> it was but a step to the decision of the SNP to put forward a motion of censure on the government for failing to bring devolution into being immediately.

But it was not only a matter of expressing dismay and disagreement. When the Nationalists put down their motion Donald Stewart, the SNP leader, expressed his hope that if the vote of No Confidence was won, and a General Election had to take place as a consequence, they would double the number of seats from the 11 they held. As for Margaret Thatcher, she could not believe her luck. After her own failed attempts at motions of censure, here was the SNP putting down their own motion, from which they could hardly retreat, and success suddenly looked a likely possibility. She was the one who moved it on the night, not any SNP MP.

That night Labour knew that all its MPs could be relied on to get themselves to Westminster in good time. They had been struggling on a day to day basis for two years after its majority had been eroded. One man, Alfred Broughton, was mortally ill, yet he was determined to get to Westminster by ambulance, not sure if he would even survive the journey. His doctors ordered him not to travel to Westminster. Despite that, Labour whips, knowing the vote was on a knife edge, urged Jim Callaghan to ask Broughton to come down, but he ruled that out. He felt it was simply wrong to impose that on anyone. Broughton died a few days later. Those were days when seriously ill MPs would get as far as the Parliament grounds in their ambulance, and have their presence checked by a whip from the other side.

The motion won by one vote. This was the first time since the Second World War that a government had lost a vote of No Confidence. The whole House saw the clerk hand the voting slip to the Conservative whip to announce the motion had won by 311 to 310.

The SNP knew Thatcher would be likely to form the next government if their motion won. Over the years since Nationalists have claimed their MPs could not have been expected to realise what the consequences of a Thatcher victory would be. They did not, they say, have a crystal ball. Well, as Nye Bevan once said, 'You don't need a crystal ball when you can read the book.' Mrs Thatcher had been strongly advocating deregulation and liberation of the market. Monetarism was her watchword. It was precisely because she promised a new beginning, very different from Ted Heath, that she was elected leader. She had made herself infamous by ending free school milk.

In the event the Nationalists lost ten seats and only one of them was re-elected along with a single gain. The Conservatives regained seven seats from the SNP. As Callaghan famously commented, never before had it been known for turkeys to vote for an early Christmas. Both Jim Sillars and John Robertson voted with the government that night, but lost their seats in the ensuing election, bringing about the final demise of the SLP.

Contrary to a myth that has been peddled since 1979, Labour did not lose support in that General Election. The Labour vote was, in fact, slightly higher than it had been in the October 1974 General Election, when Labour won more seats than the Tories. But what happened in 1979 was previously abstaining Tories flocking back to the Conservatives to give Margaret Thatcher a large majority.

We saw hard times ahead. We had to win the Council in 1980 and organise a fightback by all the Labour-controlled local authorities in the UK. I still have a copy of my leaflet from the council elections in 1980:

With the Thatcher government in power at Westminster, we must have Labour in control at the City Chambers. Glasgow cannot afford to be defenceless against Government attacks... Unemployment is now higher than at any time since the '30s. Yet government cutbacks on unemployment benefit and family allowances are going to result in £23 million less spending power in Glasgow... The new cuts in Housing mean that for every £100 spent in 1979, we are now being allowed only £40. Money is being found for tax handouts to the rich... The voters of Blairdardie will not just be registering a protest when they go out and vote Labour on May 1st. They will be supporting the only party which can put up an effective resistance... a massive vote for Labour will put heart into the movement for the long hard struggle ahead. On Glasgow District Council I will be proud to be part of it.

My SNP opponent wrote in his own leaflet, 'This ward needs a Marxist like a hole in the head.'

While all this was going on, my mother was ill in hospital, with the diagnosis of breast cancer in the late 'sixties now having spread through her system. I had been travelling to Monklands Hospital almost every day straight from work and asked them to phone me if there was any change for the worse. The day came when at work one day my colleague Calum Campbell came into the room to tell me the hospital had been on the phone and my mother had died. I kept thinking how awful it was that she had died with none of her family around her, but the ward sister told me she had slipped away in her sleep. My brother Joe had the job of arranging the funeral, and the last thing on his mind was the polling day for the municipal elections. So it transpired it was arranged for that very day. When I got around to visiting polling stations after the reception I found a SNP activist outside one of them was sneering that I had not shown my face all day, even although my son Chris had already told him I had been at my mother's funeral.

In the event I won my seat with a large majority, as did all the

Labour candidates in Garscadden, joyfully celebrating that night with Donald Dewar. The new council line-up was Labour 58 seats, Conservative 11, Liberals 3, SNP 0 – their reward for bringing in Thatcher. Throughout Scotland the results were equally satisfactory to us: Labour 469, Conservatives 232, SNP 52, Liberals 33.

The fight was on.

Chapter 13

'Raise the Scarlet Standard High'

A LITTLE KNOWLEDGE of political history is handy to have. When Margaret Thatcher ruled the roost I frequently heard cries of despair. What point was there in campaigning? She never listened to anyone. Her mantra was, 'There is no alternative.' I would point out at meeting after meeting that it was not a matter of persuading her to change her mind, the objective was to defeat her. 'Defeat her?!' people would cry. 'How can we do that?' I would remind them that within living memory Hitler's Thousand Year Reich was utterly destroyed before it reached its teens. Even the Roman Empire came to an end. I would picture a slave in ancient Roman times muttering, 'No point in protesting, Spartacus. This lot will go on and on. How could they ever be defeated?'

Then, too, the Scottish Parliament did not stand adjourned for over three centuries. It had ceased to exist. Our present Scottish Parliament is not the same Parliament 'reconvened'.

That Parliament had been a very different body from today's Scottish Parliament or the United Kingdom Parliament. It met infrequently, commonly at the behest of the monarch. It had no women members. If any woman, of any social class, had sought election to it the least she could have expected was being denounced from the pulpit by the heirs of John Knox, ranting about 'the monstrous regiment of women'. Maybe far worse. The burning of women as witches was only repealed in Scotland in 1736.

Of the men in that Parliament of over 300 years ago, not one existed who lacked title or fortune. Another two centuries were to go by before that came to pass. The domestic politics of both Scotland and England, and Great Britain when the Union was formed, were dominated by the powers of the monarchy. The religion of the monarch had been the hottest issue since the Reformation. They just did not discuss welfare, freedom from want, or equality. Even the desire to have a school in every parish was mainly about growing up to be able to read the Bible independently.

It was not about acquiring literacy so as to be able to stand up for yourself and your mates against the master, or dispute with the man in the pulpit, or express a different point of view from 'yon birkie ca'd "a lord", wha struts, an' stares, an' a' that'. We who to-day take notions of equality for granted can scarcely comprehend how startlingly brave were Robert Burns's words when he wrote his great song of defiance.

But what made me seek election to Glasgow's Council had noth-ing to do with Scottish history, ancient or modern. It was sheer rage. Rage at what Margaret Thatcher' cuts had already started doing to local services that Labour had built up.

Inflation was galloping up to over 20 per cent. Unemployment went up and kept going up. My job in the Trade Union Studies Unit made me aware of all the legislation that was going through Parliament to attack trade unions. Hundreds of shipyard workers stopped work for two hours to join health workers in a march. Miners had gone on strike in support of low paid nurses who could not take that kind of action: this was to be no longer lawful. Now strikers could be dismissed without notice, and with no right to a tribunal. Large fines, sequestration of assets, it went on and on. By the mid-'80s homeless people could be seen sleeping in shop doorways.

But first I had to get to know my ward and the organisations in it, chiefly the Community Council. I wouldn't say I got off to the best of starts. First there was the curry carry-out that someone had applied to open. Some residents objected to the smell of curry wafting around. But I knew the council had strict rules about cooking smells from commercial premises, and this was unlikely to be a problem. No one lived above the shop. I pointed out that it might turn out to be very popular, as it would save customers from taking a 20 minute bus ride to the nearest one at that time. If it proved not to be popular, then it would close. At my very first meeting, I was telling them I would not back their complaint. As it turned out, happy customers enjoyed their handy access to curries, and no smells of cooking wafted outside.

Another woman argued that single parents should not be allowed free library tickets, as they gave a bad example. I told her that it was none of the council's business how people led their lives. What I would hope was that any mother would encourage her children to use the library, which had been a great pleasure to me in my own childhood. Fortunately, everyone else disagreed with her too.

Then there was the complaint that an old man had been allocated a flat in a local block that hitherto had been reserved for elderly ladies only. But the council considered they had to be equally caring about the needs of elderly men. I cheerfully argued that having him, and some other elderly gents there, might add to the joy of life for one and all. Some of the old ladies might like to supply him with a share of their soup, or a slice of homemade cake. They had, in many cases I was sure, been used to mothering their late husbands. And he could probably help in return by wiring plugs and so on.

Donald Dewar, who had been sitting beside me at the meeting, gave me a lift home. 'Your sense of humour will be your undoing,' he remarked. But over the seven years I was Blairdardie's councillor we all got along fine. So much so that when I announced I was going to seek election to Parliament, I received a very welcome letter from the Community Council Secretary, Eric Flack, in which he said:

I consider the community has achieved a considerable amount thanks to your help. They always talked about rewiring over the last ten or so years, but when it suddenly arrived I don't think anybody was really prepared for it. Now we have reroofing and double glazing to come.

I had managed to get them their new wiring by a manoeuvre. I knew I had little hope of getting the money allocated to my area, when I wasn't in Pat Lally, the leader's gang. But I did get the Council to agree that replacement of dangerous wiring should be a priority, wherever it occurred in the city. I knew the wiring in Blairdardie houses was so old it put them right up at the top of the priority list. I had hoped the Building and Works Department would win the tender, but a firm called Lafferty's, which was used to winning an amazing proportion of the successful tenders, put in the successful bid. When the work was carried out I was incensed to see a number of households with their new switches not fitted straight but slapped on any old how. I got the Council to agree not to pay for the work until the job was done properly. And this had been supervised by a Council-employed clerk of works!

I had to struggle to get doors on the closes in my ward too. I discovered that Drumchapel closes were getting first shot at acquiring them. Fair enough, I thought, they have more problems with vandalism and strangers up to no good trespassing. Then, their doors having been vandalised, they got a second lot fitted. Then a third. My ward was still waiting to get any at all. They were good tenants in Blairdardie, who looked after their homes and gardens, and were suffering for their good citizenship. No wonder they felt aggrieved. So I had to put up a fight to get them their back doors, and in the end they got them.

I sought, and was backed by Neil Stobo, the deputy Labour leader, a strict rule that companies who had broken health and safety laws should not be invited to tender. This was followed up soon after by Neil announcing a ban on contracts with building companies who dodged taking on apprentices, and he asked me to move it at the Council meeting, where it was sure to pass with our huge Labour majority. Neil pointed out that our Direct Labour Organisation and a few private contractors were carrying the entire burden of apprenticeships. I was pleased to see Iain Dyer, Conservative housing spokesman, agreeing with us. The following year we waged war on cowboy contractors. I noted that a lot of smaller firms were not keeping up to reasonable health and safety standards for their employees, and as this enabled them to put in lower tenders it was unfair to competitors who did treat their workers more responsibly. The Council agreed to implement my amendment to standing orders accordingly. While the National Federation of Building Trades Employers agreed with our move, being eager to see us tackle firms that undercut more responsible ones, Tory Councillor Bill Aitken said, 'We will fight that idea tooth and nail.' He suspected my move was really about promoting the closed shop.

I threw myself into fighting the cuts. Glasgow District Labour Party, consisting of delegates from all the city's constituencies and affiliated trade unions, together with the Labour members of the Council, joined their efforts in the campaign.

The worst time was when the Tory government enforced compulsory competitive tendering for the work done by our Building and Works Department. No new houses were getting built, such was the severity of the cutbacks now being imposed, and so our tradesmen were all involved in repair work. Companies like Lafferty's regularly won tenders for major works, and I was worried they could drive our Building and Works Department out of existence and throw thousands of our workforce into compulsory redundancy. I didn't sleep the night before the tenders were opened, but fortunately we had won through. But the screw kept on getting tightened.

We had meetings with other Labour councillors from Stirling, Sheffield, London boroughs and the Greater London Council (GLC), and exchanged ideas. This was when I first met David Blunkett, then leader of Sheffield Council, and Ken Livingstone, Margaret Hodge and John McDonnell from London. The GLC ran an immense poster along the length of their building on the opposite side of the Thames from Parliament, much to the Tories' annoyance, showing the increasing rise in the number of unemployed in London month after month. We agreed on the 'dented shield' approach. We wouldn't do self-defeating things like set a budget without enough money to pay the wages as the end of the year approached. We wouldn't expose ourselves to personal surcharge, which meant any deemed overspend would come out of our own family's pockets. This had been tried before when councillors in Clay Cross had defied government-imposed rent rises, and their families suffered financially severely for many years while those who had cheered them on left them to pick up the tab. Neither would we resign en masse – a magnificent gesture, as the French general said of the Light Brigade, but it wasn't war.

Strathclyde Regional Council came up trumps under Charles Gray's leadership when it ran its hugely successful referendum against water privatisation, winning a turnout of voters that has never been bettered. And we still have our water safe from the profiteers.

I was only a few months on the Council when I was offered the job of depute convener of the Finance Committee, or Deputy City Treasurer, to give it its official title. At the time I wondered if I would do it well or fall on my face. When I left school and did a course in business studies, I had no interest in accountancy. This, now, was about the effective and fair running of my city. Anyway, no one was asking me to do accountancy, just understand the financial information put before me. I also knew, even in these few months I had been on the Council, that Bill English, the Finance Director, would be helpful and informative. So I thought, if I don't accept, I will look as if I am dodging responsibility. I could hear the voices, 'Oh, aye, she can criticise. But will she do anything?'

We found that some things did need shaping up. There was a great debate about closing our few remaining 'steamies', as the public wash houses were known. They are held in affectionate memory by many an aged citizen, as attested by the great popularity of Tony Roper's play, *The Steamie*, about housewives getting their washings done on Hogmanay back in the 1950s. But by the 1980s all but very few customers had stopped using them. People had washing machines and tumble dryers in their kitchens. There were coin-operated laundrettes everywhere. Bill English pointed out that the cost of running the steamies, against the income from their few customers, meant the loss to the Council was so great we would be cheaper giving each customer a present of a brand new washing machine. Call me heartless if you will, but we agreed the money saved could be better spent elsewhere on services people actually used. There was still a heated debate about it in the Labour Group on the council, and a vote to get it through. The grassroots party members thought we were only being sensible. We could have a surfeit of nostalgia in their view.

One day Bill raised his concern that the Building Department wages bill was rising month after month, and he had discovered why. It was a huge department, employing thousands of men in all the building trades. And oddly, when Thatcher's cuts were preventing us from carrying out any new build, the size of the workforce kept rising.

It turned out that Paul Mugnaioni, the recently appointed Housing Director, keen to carry out repairs on the existing housing stock, was sending more and more requests to the Building Department director for roof repairs, rewiring, new doors, and so on. He, in his turn, simply hired more and more men to keep up with the demand. At no time did it occur to him that he should mention this small matter to the finance people or any elected member.

But if left uncontrolled, it meant we were heading for the day when the money to pay wages ran out. Repairs would stop. Men who thought they had a permanent job would find themselves made redundant. The budget subcommittee were unanimous that no organisation could be allowed to run itself like that. We needed budgets for each department, expect them to stick to it, and be clear that they needed permission if they wanted to either drop or add new commitments. From now on there would be monthly reports from each department, tracing their spend as the financial year progressed, put before its departmental committee of elected members, and the Finance Committee would keep track of all of it.

Each council then was given a Housing Support Grant by central government, which was supposed to bear some relation to the size of the authority's housing stock. The amount of grant started to suffer substantial cuts, year on year, until it ceased to exist. That meant rents would have to rise. In 1980 the Government proposed we should increase our rents by 70 per cent – yes, 70 per cent! – or else drastically reduce our repairs budget. George Younger, Secretary of State for Scotland, proposed to reduce our capital allocation progressively by £1 for every £1 our rent increase fell short of the 70 per cent. The Rate Support Grant (RSG), for all expenditure that was not housing, was also cut. In 1981 George Younger took powers to withdraw RSG if expenditure was 'excessive and unreasonable'. He already had such powers, but now he could cut the grant prospectively. When councils started raising rates to compensate, they were capped. The so-called 'capital allocation' was cut. I had imagined that this phrase meant we were presented with real money for capital expenditure on building or repairing housing, libraries, baths and suchlike, as distinct from revenue spending on day to day costs like wages. Well, wouldn't most of us? If ever there was a misnomer this was it. The phrase merely meant permitted level of borrowing.

In July 1981 Younger announced action against seven Labour-controlled councils. The councils were defiant. Strathclyde region's defiance ended up with its being abolished. In 1982 the government took further powers, this time to enforce rate reductions on recalcitrant local authorities. Lothian, Stirling, Glasgow, Kirkcaldy and the Shetland Islands were to be the targets. But Shetland escaped the planned reductions, possibly because some of their elected members were prepared to block the Sullom Voe oil terminal, the major source of Britain's oil.

In Glasgow we posted a four-page newspaper to all our ratepayers, setting out our case against the government. Later on, the government took action to prevent councils from doing that. Jean McFadden suggested we wrote to all the firms we had given aid to, and to community councils, charities and voluntary bodies, asking them to write to the Secretary of State in support of their city. Many sent us copies of their letters and they made heart-warming reading.

In 1983 we drew up a Labour budget as advocated by Labour's Scottish Executive Committee and got ready to defend it to the best of our ability. We organised widespread consultation, on a departmental basis, with trade unions, tenants and community groups before final decisions were made. This degree of consultation, that people could see was not just a cosmetic exercise, and had never taken place before, reaffirmed the mandate given by the electorate in 1980 and made us able to convince the media that we had public support.

A tripartite committee was formed to campaign against the cuts. At first it consisted of trade unions, Labour councillors and party members. Later on, the Glasgow Council of Tenants joined in. This co-operation created the ability to tackle problems that could have severely affected matters for the worse. Like the day the union reps told us of departmental heads looking for cuts long before the government had even placed the Order in front of the House of Commons. The heads had thought they were merely exercising reasonable anticipation, given the huge Tory majority. Obviously, though, this had to be nipped in the bud.

Up and down the country, Labour councils got together to lobby Parliament. Sheffield, Brent, Islington, the GLC and other English councils formed a campaigning organisation. Glasgow's lobby of Parliament had magnificent support from all these councils. Sheffield party members sent a busload down at short notice to support us. Our 'war cabinet' met in Sheffield, with 22 councils represented, to campaign against the cuts in our budgets.

One of Glasgow's campaigning tactics was to print postcards, sent in their thousands, unstamped, to George Younger, who had proudly claimed that the cuts he had imposed would save the local ratepayers 19d a week. It read:

Dear Secretary of State,
As a Glasgow ratepayer I'd rather keep my city's services running than get back 19p a week. What am I supposed to do with 19p? It won't even buy half a pint of Younger's Tartan Special. I voted for good services. Please think again.

Another thing we did was put up huge posters on sites where we had planned to build council houses, saying, 'We want to build houses here. The Tory cuts are preventing it.'

I found the attitude of the Militant Tendency particularly irritating. Their line was summed up in their slogan: 'No rent rises, no rate rises, no cuts.' This defied logic. When the grants from central government were cut, you had less money to spend. Unless you put up rates and or rents. And rates were being capped by governmental diktat. Therefore, it was impossible to run any council their way without running out of money. Which was precisely what Militant wanted all councils to do. Run out of cash before the end of the financial year, and demand the government pay the wages bill.

But there was never any chance of that happening. The government had powers to take over the council in such circumstances and send in commissioners to run it as they saw fit. We would see plenty of cuts then, all right. Furthermore, the people who had voted Labour wanted us to keep things going as best as we could against the Tories, not present Thatcher with an open goal. The Militant tactic was, of course, proved spectacularly wrong in 1985 when things got so bad they had to accept help from David Blunkett, then Sheffield Council leader, to get Liverpool out of the mess they had created.

I persuaded Bob Gray, who considered himself right-wing and felt wary of the City Party members, that he should go through the budget with them and be open to hearing their views. At our first attempt at this new way of doing things – no previous City Treasurer had consulted the party – a hand rose in the air. It was one of my friends. He was frowning with concern at a line in the estimates, suggesting a 5 per cent cut in nurseries. 'Surely,' he pleaded, looking anxiously at me as he spoke, 'you cannot mean to let wee kids suffer Thatcher's cuts?'

Bob hastened to reassure him. 'It's PLANT nurseries, not under-fives nurseries. It's the regional council that runs the weans' nurseries.'

Sighs of relief all round. Who cared about plants?

In May 1982 our Tory councillors were infuriated once again by our Council holding a special meeting to express our opposition to the Falklands War, and to call for a ceasefire and a negotiated settlement through the United Nations, proposed by myself. Neil

Stobo, Deputy Leader, seconded me, saying, 'We are not prepared to sacrifice the lives of young people to save the face of this government.' The 11 Conservative and three Liberal members boycotted it. The Lord Provost, Michael Kelly, pointed out that the council's actions, such as being the first local authority to offer the freedom of the city to Nelson Mandela, had led to recognition from such bodies as the United Nations Special Committee on Apartheid. None of us, incidentally, claimed our allowance for attending this special meeting.

We had another controversy on our hands in 1982 that had nothing to do with politics, but everything to do with religion. When Pope John Paul II was due to visit our city, the Labour Group was exercised about the trees in Bellahouston Park, which would obscure people's view of the popemobile and of the altar where High Mass would be celebrated. An argument was advanced that the trees should be cut down. I thought that, if God exists, He would probably prefer to have His trees left alive to continue gracing the park for years to come. When the trees were cut down the Orange Lodge complained it was because there were too many Catholics on the council, but in reality there were many who simply wanted people to enjoy a once in a lifetime event, and be able to see His Holiness, and they cared little about the trees.

Then, in August, the Tory opposition on the Council exploded in fury when I cancelled a meeting of a Finance subcommittee so that I and fellow councillors, as well as any of the workforce who were free, could support a NHS workers' demonstration going on outside our windows in George Square. The demo was supported by delegations from steel works, shipyards and other industries. People could do that before the Thatcher changes in labour law came into force. Councillor Bill Aitken, Tory Group leader, said, 'The leftward drift of the Labour Group is becoming alarming.' There was only one item on the agenda, and it could easily wait until the meeting of the parent committee. I was actually saving the ratepayers' money, as no allowances could be claimed for a cancelled meeting.

By 1983 I was raising the subordinate position of women in

Scottish society. There were only eight women out of 57 in the Labour Group on my own council. I persuaded the Council to agree to set up a working party including the trade unions to review recruitment, promotion and opportunities for women at all levels. But what really upset Bill Aitken was my move two years before that to put the words 'Glasgow District Council is an Equal Opportunities Employer' on all our job advertisements. By 1984 we had a job sharing scheme, the first run by any Scottish Council.

And still we had to fight Militant while fighting the Tories. The National Union of Students' Conference held a debate in Blackpool one night, at 10.00pm, of all the unlikely hours. Militant supporters were, as usual, praising Liverpool's council and rubbishing all others. I was billed to speak on behalf of Labour in Glasgow.

'Do you support Liverpool cutting the rents?' a voice in the crowd shouted to me.

'Something I do agree with them on,' I replied. 'Under the previous Liberal administration, they had been much too high.'

I could guess what was coming. 'So why doesn't Glasgow cut their rents then?'

I replied, 'Glasgow does not believe it can do so in current circumstances and attempt to keep up with essential repairs.'

'Shame! Disgrace! Call yourselves socialists!' the cry went up from Militant supporters all around the hall.

'Perhaps I should explain. Liverpool rents now stand at an average of £19. Glasgow's are £14.'

Militant never gained much support in Glasgow. I attribute that to the common sense of my fellow citizens, but it must be said it was much the same throughout Scotland. They were simply laughed out of existence. In the '80s a huge contribution to their humiliation was made by the members of the Red Review, a troupe of members of Glasgow University Labour Club, the leading lights being John and Richard Beal. Their shows at party conferences brought the house down as they parodied all sorts of idiocies afflicting the party at that time, and Militant was a target they never missed. Militant were always claiming their Marxist analysis would solve all problems. They began to sound like a washing powder ad as they advocated their Bold Socialist Programme as the answer to everything. One song went:

When Sunny Jim and Michael Foot
tried to sort the crisis oot
they didnae know what the problem wis
'cause they hadnae got a Marxist analysis.

Of course, their notion of a Marxist analysis was whatever their guru Ted Grant said, which they swallowed with all the critical discernment of a fish imbibing plankton. Whenever *Militant* 'readers' (they always denied they had members) claimed they had a Marxist analysis of a problem this was never intended as a contribution to how the difficulty might realistically be resolved. It was a way of making themselves sound clever and well-informed. But you have to wonder if satire can compete with the Militant-supporting community worker who told a tenant she hadn't got the repair to her window done because of the crisis of capitalism and the Council not having a Marxist analysis of the situation.

Boris Johnson, when he came up here and debated these matters with me on television after I had become an MP, argued that capital had been thrown at Glasgow. At that time, I did not know who he was. Here was this Tory guy, with a mop of unruly blond hair, waving his arms about and asserting Glasgow got loads of money for our houses. He was so animated, jumping up and down in his seat, I really do believe he did not understand, and was not trying to deceive the viewers. I offered to take him round my own constituency, where closes in Milton had not had a lick of paint in 40 years. To which he said, well, couldn't they do it themselves?

It was demanding tackling the council's finances, both in terms of time consumed night after night, getting directors to 'sharpen their pencils' and getting the political task accomplished.

I loved doing the work of Deputy Treasurer for four years and felt I had earned my promotion to be the next City Treasurer after Bob Gray became Lord Provost in 1984. I would have been the first female one in the city's history. It never occurred to me that

Pat Lally would want the job, but it was a step towards the leadership and ousting Jean McFadden. In due course he defeated Jean by means of sympathetic arms around shoulders when Jean, determined to run a tight ship, had taken to task any councillor who had done anything that could bring us into disrepute.

Pat then set up a Tribune Group which had no connection whatsoever with that left-wing Labour activists' weekly. His aim was simply to undermine Jean and present a Left front to the more naive party members. I refused to have anything to do with it.

But first he had to achieve getting the job of City Treasurer. His supporters even put it about that I didn't want the job. Nothing could have been further from the truth. But Jean's camp was defeated by his camp. He had the votes, and he got the job. I was offered the convenorship of the Manpower Committee. I accepted, on condition it changed its name to Personnel Committee. Then the fun began.

Chapter 14

'Which Side Are You On?'

IN MARCH 1984 as co-ordinator of the Hands Off Glasgow campaign, I represented our council at a rally for the miners during their year-long strike. The star speaker was Tony Benn.

Our council gave licences for street collections for the miners. Many of us did collections every Saturday morning all that year. We told the firms that supplied us that any companies crossing picket lines would be blacked from quoting for our contracts. A caravan was sited in George Square to collect food and money. The white collar union, NALGO, distributed collecting cans wherever they worked in all our public buildings. Councillor Madge O'Neill made a weekly collection from fellow councillors that raised over £10,000 in total. Our council donated £20,000 to the Lord Provost of Edinburgh's appeal fund for miners' families.

The Tories enforced further cuts upon us. Six months after every council's budget was set, and their rates levied to bring in the necessary income, they cut £90 million off the RSG to all these councils, in the hope of axing their programmes and enforcing cuts. But the Labour councils got together, and in common with every other Labour Council in Scotland, Glasgow refused to cut its budget or put up the rents.

The work Glasgow was getting done – £8 millon worth – would deal with only some of the worst cases of dampness, asbestos and dangerous wiring. The tenants needed it. Building workers needed the jobs. Yet the state had – and still has – an impressive array of law to deter councils from disobedience: every councillor can be held personally responsible for his or her share of the illegal expenditure, barred from holding public office and finally jail.

Strathclyde Regional Council provided free school meals for striking miners' children. Both councils had been warned the Government would take action against us for spending council funds in such ways, but we defied them and got away with it.

One night a *Big, Big Show* was put on at the King's Theatre in support of the miners. On stage to entertain us were John Cairney, Andy Cameron, Dick Gaughan, Anne Lorne Gillies, Carol Kidd, Phil McCall, Bill McCue, Chic Murray, Peggy O'Keefe, Wildcat and 7:84. But the act that brought the house down was a troupe of firefighters parodying the Chippendales. Dressed in full gear, they danced to 'Big Spender' while divesting themselves of their boots, socks, trousers, tunics and so on. Then, as the heavy beats of 'The Stripper' came to an end, they held their helmets strategically in front of them and ran off into the wings. Unforgettable.

But as we all know, in the end the miners were defeated. Of all the sights of the 1980s, the one that above all sticks in my mind is the Welsh miners marching back to their pits, heads held high and banners aloft. I am not easily moved to tears, but tears poured down my face as I watched that news bulletin.

When I became Convener of Glasgow District Council's Personnel Committee in 1984 I was determined to pursue the equality agenda vigorously. Under our 'Ability not Disability' policy, the Council would now state 'all vacancies are open to suitably qualified disabled people' in all our press advertisements for jobs. The GMWU appealed on behalf of a member who worked in our nursery gardens, and whose manager wanted to sack him on account of persistent late coming. He was a capable and conscientious worker. But his deafness meant he could not hear his alarm clock. Not even three alarm clocks. On our committee's instructions, one of the personnel department officials looked into possible solutions, and discovered there was such a thing as a small plastic instrument that vibrated enough to wake the dead, and if placed under a pillow would do the trick. The man kept his job.

The following month I slated our Parks Department for condemning hundreds of manual workers to miserable conditions, huddling together in shanty huts in bad weather. A report by officials showed huts had no facilities to dry out clothing that had got soaked in the rain; of four lights in one bothy, not one was working; and the kitchens were in such a bad state they needed gutted – they were beyond improvement and repair. I was shocked when I discovered all this and raised it successfully with the Parks Committee. The entire Personnel Committee had been equally appalled at what we had learned. But I had to think, how could it come about that a Labour council could put itself in line for this entirely fair criticism?

Other problems were flagged up. The Equal Opportunities Working Party had tried to include gays and lesbians in our equal opportunities policy, and failed. The Labour Group voted 34 to 14 against, arguing the phrase 'no discrimination on grounds of sex' was sufficient to cover the matter, when it clearly was not.

I tried to gain same sex partners the same rights as heterosexual couples on time off for funerals. It seemed to me grossly unfeeling not to recognise sorrow for the loss of a partner, and that it was immaterial whether their loved one was of the same sex or not. It was defeated at a meeting of the local authorities' employers' side on the grounds that it would be too costly! At one such meeting of the employers' side, and the first one where I was representing Glasgow District Council, I had to deal with a sexist chairman who kept calling speakers, twice in some cases, without calling me. My hand was held up so long my arm was getting sore. But no way was he going to get away with ignoring Glasgow. At last he said, turning to me with an indulgent smile, 'And what have you got to say, darling?'

I answered between gritted teeth, 'I thought you'd never ask, sweetheart.' He didn't do that again.

But the big issue was sex discrimination in pay. Male manual workers' earnings were in all cases higher than the earnings of women manual workers. The women who looked after the highly valuable paintings hanging in the City Chambers were paid far less than the men who hosed down the backsides of the highland cattle in Pollok Park. A level of skill that required no training whatsoever, except possibly in leaping fences to escape from an angry bull.

Then in the course of auditing a local housing office's accounts it was discovered that someone called wee Annie did the dusting, polishing and vacuuming, and was paid from the petty cash box. No, they had no idea there was a proper rate per hour for her job, and that they had been underpaying her for years. My committee agreed that Annie should be back paid in full.

Then there was the clerkess who had been put on a manual grading although she was employed to do clerical work. A senior official had done this to circumvent a council decision to limit the number of white collar staff. Instead of earning £5,052 a year, she was paid the kitchen assistant wage of £4,288. My committee were incensed, and insisted on her being back paid in full, with a letter of apology.

After these episodes I got the Council to agree to a review of pay grades, in co-operation with all the relevant unions, on a promise that no individual worker would suffer financial loss if any job were downgraded. But we could not implement this on our own. We had to get COSLA (the Convention of Scottish Local Authorities) to agree, and they eventually did. Then it went to a meeting of representatives of all the local authorities in Britain. They also agreed, provided it was implemented in stages as the cost of redressing these imbalances would be enormous. The unions accepted that an equal value specialist consultant should oversee the job evaluation exercise under way, and we agreed criteria.

It was all the more disturbing, therefore, when I discovered some years ago that matters had deteriorated. Women were discovering that men who were members of their own union had been getting bonuses that put them ahead of the female members. These bonuses were not for extra work. Nor for exceptional work. They were paid just for turning up. I was furious. It was only discovered when some women went to lawyers for advice about the Equal Pay Act and started raising actions in court. Then – the nerve of it! – the women were accused of risking the jobs of all their fellow workers if councils had to pay out. There have been substantial cases of restoration back to equal pay, but it is not fully resolved yet. The women's strike in 2018, backed up by so many male colleagues refusing to cross picket lines, has given heart to the whole trade union movement.

1984 was the year in which the Council started to take on girl school leavers as apprentices. Three, to be precise. Two joiners, one painter. Still, it was a start. It was the first time the Council's Building and Works Department had taken on young women to train for a trade. When I first mooted the idea of opening up apprenticeships to female school leavers it was hardly a revolutionary idea. I had been teaching female apprentice electricians in the mid-'70s. Yet at a meeting of the Personnel Committee almost a decade later, a trade union full time official demurred. He said he couldn't see how that would work.

'Why don't you think so?' I asked.

'Well,' said he, 'most of these young women will probably get married in due course.'

'I expect so. What's that got to do with it?'

'Well, Councillor, I think you may not realise that work starts early in the morning on building sites.'

'Of course I do. So why is that a problem?'

'Well, how could she make her man's breakfast?'

So he could do his job, but not do that onerous task all by himself?

Then on another day later on I asked Brian Gallagher, the Director of the Building and Works Department, why there were still hardly any young women amongst the new apprentices. He replied, with an irritating smirk, that there was a practical problem we had failed to consider. There were no female toilets on their building sites.

'Let me get this right,' I said. 'You have a workforce of around four thousand. You have plumbers, electricians, joiners, bricklayers and painters. And you are telling me you can't build a ladies' toilet?' Bob Gray, the Lord Provost, was sitting at my side. Added to which, Bob had been a clerk of works, and had taught building trades in one of the city's further education colleges.

'Better do what Councillor Fyfe says,' he said, laughing, 'and no, you're not getting any more money. Out of your present budget, just for your cheek.'

The anti-cuts campaign in Glasgow was still going strong. The RSG kept getting cut and was now down to 56.1 per cent. Housing Support Grant was cut from £213 million in 1979 to £50.7 million in 1986, and finally withdrawn altogether.

Then the Labour Group adopted a policy that could have done untold harm to our fightback. In December 1986 the Group's executive committee recommended that the post of Director of Building and Works should be tested on the market, and that Mr Gallagher should be invited to apply, with a guarantee he would be shortlisted. But he had a three year fixed term contract. In January 1987 NALGO blacklisted the post. In March the Personnel subcommittee on appeals, chaired by my vice-convener Councillor Alex Mosson, upheld Gallagher's appeal. The sub tied four – four. Alex used his casting vote in favour of the appeal, and I was one of those who supported it. Gallagher would not now have to compete with others for his own job, and then be rejected.

The Labour Group could not, under our own rules, instruct our subcommittee how to decide on the appeal. But what they proposed was inappropriate for a good employer – and my job at the Central College of Commerce was lecturing on TUC courses for union reps, including advice on how to tackle employers doing this kind of thing. I simply could not do it myself. If I did I would have to resign from my job at Central College's Trade Union Studies Unit, and in disgrace at that. To get rid of Gallagher, they could simply not renew his contract when it ended or sack him if they thought the grounds were serious enough to break the contract. Instead what they wanted Gallagher to do was waive his rights to appeal against any future decision not to renew his contract, and if he refused to do so his appointment would be terminated forthwith. I could see an Employment Tribunal having fun with that. The Group were so furious with Alex and me they removed Alex from the vice-convenership of the Personnel Committee and even membership of that committee. It was merely a reprimand for me considering that, by that time, I was the Labour candidate for Maryhill in the forthcoming General Election. This ensured a big row at the City Labour Party meeting, where they vigorously supported Alex and me in an emergency motion. One delegate even compared our stand to Galileo's.

As for the unions, they were rightly furious. NALGO called a meeting of all the unions with members employed by the council. They argued, 'This business has damaged, possibly destroyed, the whole credibility of the appeals procedure. What is the point in the trade unions taking a case to the appeals committee, if the Labour Group, as employer, has already taken the decision behind closed doors to sack someone?' I couldn't have agreed more. And further, all this was happening when we were supposed to be uniting to fight Thatcher's cuts.

In the end, Brian Gallagher, just before the deadline, signed a new contract accepting waiving his right of appeal. A new standing order was approved, giving the Council the final say in matters relating to personnel appeals.

It is commonplace nowadays for large employers to have equal opportunities staff. Back in 1985, when the Council decided to appoint its first one, there was quite a stushie. Jess Fitzgerald was, simply, the best of the candidates. The fact that she was also the wife of Labour councillor Eamonn Fitzgerald was irrelevant. Eamonn was not a member of any relevant committee.

We had created the post because, out of 768 senior posts, only 50 were occupied by women. Furthermore, in a workforce of 14,000, only 57 were of ethnic minorities. We planned to monitor each department for its success – or lack of it – in redressing the balance. Application forms were to be designed so as to prevent bias against a candidate, so no more questions like, 'Which school did you attend?' When Jim Weir, the Personnel Director, had to attend COSLA meetings he would ruefully explain he was henpecked by Jean and me.

Trying to be good employers, our Equal Opportunities Working Party proposed having a crèche for council workers' children. Pat Lally opposed it on the grounds that the ratepayers would object.

Eventually I managed to get a sum put in the estimates for the creation of a crèche. Yippee! But I cheered too soon. Pat objected to every proposal for a site to place the nursery, and eventually the commitment was dropped after I left the council.

There were other aspects of being a Glasgow councillor that come back to haunt me. The Licensing Committee decided to inspect a performance of a belly dancer at a new Turkish restaurant. The convener came back and reported that, while the dance was perfectly decent, he could not understand why she had to dance in bare feet.

An Indian temple in the West End had a bell, to which some local residents objected. We tested the decibel level and found it far quieter than the church bells ringing nearby on a Sunday morning. Complaint dismissed.

Meanwhile other stuff was going on in my life. As an active member of the Labour Co-ordinating Committee (LCC) I was elected to the Labour Party's Scottish Executive in 1982, and started to get involved in local government issues, political education and the women's committee. The LCC believed in imaginative and energetic campaigning, while recognising reality and not pretending constraints did not exist.

In 1985 I had the great good fortune to be chosen to be Labour's candidate for Glasgow Maryhill for the forthcoming General Election. This had been entirely unexpected. The seats of Maryhill and Kelvingrove had been merged in 1983, and Jim Craigen was sure to hold on to the new Maryhill. He had been the old Maryhill's MP for several years, and Maryhill members were, on the whole, traditionalist in their attitudes and somewhat deferential to their MP. Kelvingrove members had a much higher ratio of people with academic qualifications, and they were anything but deferential. They tended to be left-wing, Maryhill right-wing. Many of the Kelvingrove people were unhappy with Jim, but only a small minority wanted to deselect him. Jim earned respect for the good work he did on housing. This was a time when there was a lot of tension between party members and some of the MPs. We could see that no matter how unsatisfactory an MP was, there was no way of shifting him. The last straw was the London Newham MP, Reg Prentice, who treated his local party with contempt. The local members were helpless. They were proved to be in the right when he crossed the floor of the House and joined the Tories. Enough. The rules were changed so that MPs could be reselected or deselected. This caused worry to MPs who were out of tune with their local parties. I knew Jim Craigen was not in danger, and said so to Bob Gray who was one of his closest supporters. The vast majority of the left-wingers were a decent bunch and did not want to go so far as to throw a man out of his job. They only wanted as good a relationship as possible. If Jim would turn up at our meetings, and send reports when he could not, that would help. Labour was not expecting to win the next election and Jim, I was told much later, did not want to spend another four or five years in opposition, when he felt he could do work of positive value in housing, and so to everyone's surprise he announced he was standing down and would not seek re-election. We had to find a candidate in 1985 for a General Election that could not be more than two years away and could be any time Mrs Thatcher decided.

I had already expressed my willingness to fight a hopeless seat for Labour somewhere or other, but when this turn of events occurred I thought, well, why not try for this safe seat where I actually live?

I went to see Hugh Wyper, the head man of the Transport and General Workers' Union in Scotland, which I had joined some years before. He said to me, 'They'll never pick you in Maryhill. They're too right-wing.' I pointed out that things had changed, and I might have a chance. I knew the T&G would choose one person to support in any one constituency, and George Galloway would be sure to try for their backing in Maryhill. He had already tried with T&G backing, without success, in one or two other seats. I then went through the T&G's winnowing procedure, which began with an interview with their Scottish Finance and General Purposes Committee. I was amazed and overwhelmed when these tough-minded men actually rose to their feet to applaud at the end. Then it was off to London for the UK equivalent. I was ushered into a room, where two long rows of men sat facing each other, and I was seated at the far end. Not one of them gave anything away as they sat, poker-faced, making notes as I answered their questions. I was later told I had passed with flying colours, and the union was delighted to be in the forefront of helping Labour women get selected as candidates for safe seats next time round. I was to be on their A List, which meant they would give much-needed supporting funding to my Constituency Labour Party (CLP). Not that I was allowed, under party rules, to mention that in my efforts to get selected. Ron Todd, the General Secretary, sent me a warm congratulatory letter. All this meant I could rely on support from the GMB and NUPE as well.

There were five people shortlisted. Robin Stewart, a teacher and former European candidate, was the Co-operative Party nominee. Danny Crawford had lived in the area all his life and was highly regarded. Jim Mackechnie, a librarian and outstanding Strathclyde Regional Councillor, an old friend of my husband Jim and mine from our wasted year in Sillars' SLP, had quite a lot of left-wing support but, I believed, was not likely to win through. And not just because of Maryhill right-wingers. He had reason to believe that those in the breakaway sect from the IMG put up Chris Aldred to attack him for having left them several years before. This sect used aliases to make it more difficult for the security services to track them down, and one comrade was furious with Jim Mackechnie for, at a meeting one night, forgetfully calling him by his real name.

While I recognised that everyone had a right to support whoever they liked, I was disappointed that the women's section nominated Chris. I had been working for women as a member of the Council, achieving progress in equal opportunities and equal pay. But Chris attacked this record because Glasgow only had an equal opportunities subcommittee and not a women's committee. I had figured that if my fellow councillors would not agree to having a women's committee I could settle for equal opportunities as the committee's name and do the same things anyway. Chris was so critical of the Labour Party I wondered why she was a member. At one of our meetings she claimed the Labour Party was racist, and I wasn't having that. I said if I thought that, I wouldn't be a member.

There was a split amongst the various Trots. Happily for me, some were impressed by the fact I had been blacklisted by Singers several years before, for exposing their dishonesty. They were urging moderation in pay claims because we were in competition with the Far East, while they themselves were opening factories in eastern countries. When Ian Davidson and Des McNulty, the leaders of my campaign, were helping me to compose my CV, Ian asked me about my trade union history. I mentioned the blacklisting as a humorous aside, thinking it was of no consequence because it had never actually done me any harm, but they both said, 'You've got to put that in. Anyone can say they were Secretary of this, or Chair of that, but this is something the rest of them can't say.'

Maryhill members decided on a very demanding procedure to select its candidate. First, we were interviewed at each of the three local branches. Second, all the nominees had to pore through the Maryhill CLP policy book and to answer whether we supported each policy or not, and if not, why not. When I went through the book with Des and Ian, I wondered aloud why I found it so easy to agree with nearly all of it. Des laughed. 'Well, that's because you won the arguments.' Third, we had an Any Questions panel of the nominees, open to all members, not just those who had a vote at the selection conference. Lastly, on the day for selection, each nominee made a short speech followed by questions from the floor. These questions are seldom from simple seekers of information. They are usually designed as traps they hope a candidate they don't support will fall into, and better still, be beneficial to the candidate they do want.

On the afternoon of the selection conference, chaired by Jimmy Allison the Scottish Organiser and attended by 60 delegates, it came down to a final run-off between Danny and me. To my surprise I won.

One argument that I believe clinched it for me was that those voting knew, if I did not win, Labour would have not one female candidate in a winnable seat in the whole of Scotland. Women in the party were fed up with there having only ever been nine women Labour MPs in Scotland. More men were voted in as new Labour

MPs in every General Election. In selecting me Maryhill did strike out and make a difference. I ended up being the sole female out of our group of 50 Scottish Labour MPs. This was incredible good luck, being selected for one of Labour's safest seats at my first attempt.

On Friday 4 July 1986 my younger son, Chris, graduated at Strathclyde University at the age of 19. Jim had been feeling out of sorts for a few days, so much so he had a struggle to get out of bed to go to the graduation ceremony. He thought it was indigestion, and as he was always buying Rennies tablets, and refusing to take time to go and see the doctor, I just thought this was the same as usual. On the Saturday night I sent for a doctor because by this time it was clear there was something badly wrong. The wall of his stomach was stretched tight like a drum. The locum who came gave him a prescription, and we still had no idea what was wrong. On the Monday morning, when he seemed no better, I insisted we went down to the surgery, which was just a short walk away. Dr White, as soon as he saw Jim, phoned the Western Infirmary and told me to get him there in a taxi from the rank outside, and not wait for an ambulance. They operated on him soon after, and I was told he had 32 pints of blood poured into him. That night I sat by his hospital bedside, by then realising he was in danger of death. But it seemed incredible. Big, strong men like Jim, who never had anything wrong with them except a touch of indigestion, didn't die. But he did, at the age of 45, at 10.00am on the Tuesday morning. It was an abdominal haemorrhage, and Dr White told me later it was an aneurysm, just waiting to burst. He could have dropped dead any time.

Jim had lived his life with great zest. He had a favourite saying, 'a short life and a merry one'. He certainly had his wish. In the following months my sons Stephen and Chris were my rocks. I had not realised they could be so mature. My brother Jim flew from Los Angeles to comfort me. I will always be grateful to my chums, especially Johann, for insisting on getting me out, even if only for a few drinks in the pub and a chat, or a curry, and refusing to take 'No' for an answer. My brother Joe had only a few months before lost his own wife, Margaret, to cancer, and she too had died in her

40s. That brought Joe and me closer together.

But you have to get on with life. I was glad I had so much to do, in my job, as a councillor and as a Parliamentary candidate. It stopped me from staying in, staring at the walls. Then, when I became an MP, I came across plenty of constituents whose lives would drive many to despair. I sometimes heard of such appalling circumstances in people's lives it was all I could do to remain dry-eyed listening to them. But I felt anger, too, that people coping with great difficulties often lacked the help that a better ordered society would never grudge them. We have only got one life, so it's hard that for too many people it is far from being a merry one.

Even today, all these years later, I still hear people reminiscing about Jim as a journalist, NUJ activist and political animal. Our Labour Party branch in North Kelvin/Woodlands put out a branch bulletin with a farewell on its front page headed, 'Goodbye, Jim'. At the end of the biographical notes written by Andrew Hargrave, the doyen of the Glasgow journalists, he commented:

Although he rarely took party office, his voice was often heard at meetings – usually from the back of the hall – urging, cautioning, warning, questioning. Often he carried on the discussion after meetings with friends, colleagues and comrades over a pint, always with his keen sense of the ridiculous. He was good company, and we shall miss him.

That was the Labour family gathering round. It meant a lot to me. As the days went on towards the coming General Election I was thinking how much my experience both with the trade union movement and our city council had made it possible for me to be one of the few ever Labour women MPs. I owed them. I looked forward to sticking up for them. And there was another battle to be fought – equal representation of women. The indomitable Judith Hart was standing down, and that meant I was likely to be – as she had been – the sole female Labour MP in Scotland. Judith commented to me, 'You don't know what you're letting yourself in for.' How right she was. But that's another story.

Postscript

WHEN WRITING THIS book I recounted stories about education, work, holidays and local government. Today I would be looking at chaos in education, jobs going day after day, holidays subject to the vagaries of a virus, and local authorities so drained of finance they are near collapse. We need competent, caring government at all levels. It won't fall out of the sky. We need to vote for it.

Let's begin by focusing on our relations with the USA. It is obvious that the 'special relationship' is a myth. The POTUS has made that pretty clear, because he lacks the statecraft of his predecessors in skirting around it. It was always the case. Remember Grenada? The USA was opposed to its government, so their soldiers were sent in without even bothering to tell Margaret Thatcher, at that time the UK Prime Minister, who had assumed until then that any part of the Commonwealth was inviolate. An independent Scotland is not likely to be too extreme for American tastes, we needn't fear a Bay of Pigs or repeated attempts to assassinate Nicola Sturgeon. But ridding ourselves of Trident in an independent Scotland would not go down well at all. Trident is not independent. That's American missiles being stored at Faslane. The least we could expect is rather tougher negotiations on trade deals, while already as we are now we have to try to defend Scottish products from worsening conditions for entry to their market. So a good step now would be to call for support for the Treaty Prohibiting Nuclear Weapons, which both the USA and UK have refused to sign.

Barack Obama has observed that Donald Trump doesn't do the job of President because he can't. This is proved day after day. Here is a man who mocks Joe Biden for wearing a face mask, and two days later he is in hospital needing an oxygen mask. He has even asserted that postal votes should be discounted because of fraud, for which he has provided no evidence. This clearly shows he is out to dispute a Joe Biden victory and would not accept a transfer of power. Already there are blocks on black citizens' ability to cast their votes that should not exist in any country that calls itself a democracy. It's in all our interests that Trump is defeated, well and soundly.

Then there's Brexit. We are now out of the EU, and at time of writing have still not concluded negotiations with this huge trading partner. It is quite possible we will end up out on our own. People who wanted out on left wing grounds, correctly criticising the EU for policies like forbidding state aid to industries in difficulties, are confronted with poorer working conditions imposed by a government that wanted the freedom to do exactly that. On top of that our government is openly ready to break international law. American politicians declare there will be no trade agreement with the UK if the Good Friday Agreement is put in jeopardy. Looks as if Number 10 is even more clueless than we thought. They have contrived to put us out of Europe and place our futures in the hands of the USA.

So now look at the UK. The Tories have abolished England's public health body with no consultation. The exams system for all four nations is in chaos. The economy in recession, jobs going by the thousands. Our very democracy is under threat. The attempt to prorogue Parliament was defeated in the courts, but now Parliament is being sidelined anyway. We've got to fight back. This is no time to stand aside, saying they're all the same. How much clearer can it be made that they are not?

Thinking about all the above, where should Scotland stand? The polls show rising support for independence. Yet Nicola Sturgeon is right to want fuller, longer commitment because if a second attempt at a referendum is made, and loses, it will stay lost for a very long time. It is to be hoped that the SNP will consider, before seeking this huge change, the substantial problems for which they will need answers.

At present she benefits – as does her party – from daily broadcasts as the mother of the nation, telling us the latest about the virus. At least she sounds coherent, unlike Johnson. I do not call for her to be silenced, on the contrary, I want to hear her answers to the Salmond enquiry, whose efforts to establish who knew what and when are being frustrated. What is lacking is simply space for the other parties too. Isn't the BBC supposed to give balance? Although she gets media questions, the BBC seldom provides opportunities for other parties to have their say. There is much else to talk about that gets hardly any airing. That will change in the run-up to polling day, but it should change right now. The SNP has still to spell out what currency we would have. There are a whole range of issues that are outside the remit of the Scottish Parliament, but will have to be addressed as best they can when seeking support for their breakaway. Waving the Saltire doesn't answer any questions.

All of which makes me more convinced than ever that there are plenty of people who seek evidence before deciding. Judging by number of votes cast (always less noticeable than seats won and lost) Labour was actually far from doom in 2019 but that never gets noted. Don't wonder why. Boris Johnson's existence is not a reason to change the whole future of our country. He's not immortal. He may not even last much longer as Prime Minister, given the dissatisfaction openly expressed by Tory MPs. I make no bones I have always thought that Scotland breaking away does not guarantee a better life for all, and in fact it has already been admitted we could be in for tough times for the first ten years. We all know who the tough times always hit hardest. But that can and must change. Remember how much Mary Barbour's army achieved, and they didn't even have the vote. I have often had it remarked to me, 'If only we had a Mary Barbour today.' I always respond, 'We can all try to have a little of Mary Barbour in us.'

Let's go to it!

Luath Press Limited

committed to publishing well written books worth reading

LUATH PRESS takes its name from Robert Burns, whose little collie Luath (*Gael.*, swift or nimble) tripped up Jean Armour at a wedding and gave him the chance to speak to the woman who was to be his wife and the abiding love of his life. Burns called one of the 'Twa Dogs' Luath after Cuchullin's hunting dog in Ossian's *Fingal*. Luath Press was established in 1981 in the heart of Burns country, and is now based a few steps up the road from Burns' first lodgings on Edinburgh's Royal Mile. Luath offers you distinctive writing with a hint of unexpected pleasures.

Most bookshops in the UK, the US, Canada, Australia, New Zealand and parts of Europe, either carry our books in stock or can order them for you. To order direct from us, please send a £sterling cheque, postal order, international money order or your credit card details (number, address of cardholder and expiry date) to us at the address below. Please add post and packing as follows: UK – £1.00 per delivery address; overseas surface mail – £2.50 per delivery address; overseas airmail – £3.50 for the first book to each delivery address, plus £1.00 for each additional book by airmail to the same address. If your order is a gift, we will happily enclose your card or message at no extra charge.

ILLUSTRATION: IAN KELLAS

Luath Press Limited
543/2 Castlehill
The Royal Mile
Edinburgh EH1 2ND
Scotland
Telephone: +44 (0)131 225 4326 (24 hours)
Email: sales@luath. co.uk
Website: www.luath.co.uk